BARCELONA

A CITY AND ITS ARCHITECTURE

An Essay by Josep Maria Montaner

TASCHEN

KÖLN LISBOA LONDON NEW YORK PARIS TOKYO

This book was printed on 100 % chlorine-free bleached paper in accordance with the TCF-standard.

© 1997 Benedikt Taschen Verlag GmbH
Hohenzollernring 53, D-50672 Köln
Edited, designed and produced by Gabriele Leuthäuser, Nuremberg
Text of illustrations by Verónica Reisenegger, Cologne; Peter H. Untucht,
Freiburg; Josep Maria Montaner, Barcelona
English translation by Michael Scuffil, Leverkusen
Cover design: Angelika Taschen, Cologne

Printed in Spain
ISBN 3-8228-9653-5
GB

CONTENTS

TOWARDS THE EIXAMPLE

LA CASA DE LA CIUTAT (left)

Pere Llobet, 1373; Arnau Bargués,
1399–1402; Josep Mas i Vila, 1831–1847
Plaça de Sant Jaume

PALAU DE LA GENERALITAT

Marc Safont, 1416–1434; Pere Blay,
1596–1617
Plaça de Sant Jaume

In the well-preserved Gothic section of the mediaeval City Hall, the Casa de la Ciutat, is the Saló de Cent. It was here that centuries ago the "Council of One Hundred" gathered to debate the future of Catalonia. The damage resulting from the War of the Spanish Succession in 1714 and that caused by a bomb attack in 1842 led to the precautionary demolition of part of the structure. In the early 20th century, however, a decision was taken not only to renovate the building, but also to enlarge it.

The Saló de Cent, the "Hall of the Hundred", with its splendid chandeliers and its broad round arches, is reminiscent of a church. This impression is reinforced by the arrangement of the pew-like wooden benches: semicircular at the front of the room for the political dignitaries and parallel rows – set clearly apart – for their followers.

Directly opposite this City Hall, the Ajuntament, is the Palau de la Generalitat, the residence of the Catalan presidents; it is as if the political antagonists – regional governor on the one hand, mayor of the city on the other – did not wish to lose sight of each other. The regional seat of government was begun at the beginning of the 15th century and enlarged on several occasions since. The multi-sectioned complex between the Carrer de la Ciutat, the Carrer dels Templers and the Plaça de Sant Miquel contains, alongside the Saló Daurat, or Gilded Hall, the lofty belfry. The southern section of the palace, facing on to the Plaça de Sant Jaume, was designed by Pere Blay in the late 16th century and is regarded as one of the most successful examples of Renaissance architecture in Barcelona.

PORTA DE SANTA MADRONA
Avinguda del Parallel

However meagre the remains of the fortified city walls when compared with their original extent, they are nevertheless testaments to Barcelona's urban expansion. Fragments dating from many centuries mark the stages in the city's expansion, from the mediaeval town with its defensive ramparts to the "boundless" metropolis of the industrial age. The tower near the sea dates back to the middle of the 13th century – like the oldest part of the wall – and once formed part of the Drassanes,

the former shipyard, built under Peter the Great. Approximately 100 years later, the Raval district was provided with defences in the form of a new ring of fortifications following the course of the present-day Ronda, at the end of which a second tower was constructed, which served at the same time as a city gate, the Porta de Santa Madrona. The section of wall connecting the two towers dates from the 17th century, when the expansion of the Drassanes required a more substantial

form of protection. To this end, the same century saw the construction of the Baluarde de Santa Madrona, a bulwark which necessitated straightening out the old city wall. Finally, the 18th century saw the construction of the Baluarde of Próspero de Verboom, whose purpose was also strategic, aiming to transform the Drassanes into a citadel.

PALAU REIAL MAJOR

Guillem Carbonell, 1359–1370; Antoni
Carbonell, 1546–1549; Joaquim Vilaseca i
Rivera, Adolf Florensa i Ferrer, 1936–1956
Plaça del Rei

The massive complex of buildings around
the Plaça del Rei was once the seat of the
Counts of Barcelona and centuries before
that, in all probability, a residence of the
Visigoth kings. Three buildings in this
monumental ensemble are worthy of espe-
cial mention: the Palau Reial Major, built
on Roman foundations and restored and
enlarged several times, the first occasion
being in the early 12th century under
Ramon Berenguer IV. Between 1359 and
1370, the Gothic Saló del Tinell was

added, where Christopher Columbus
would be received by the Catholic mon-
archs Ferdinand of Aragon and Isabella of
Castile after his return from America in
1493. The second significant building is
the small Gothic Capella de Santa Ague-
da, dating from the 14th century, and the
third is the Palau del Lloctinent, the
"lieutenant's palace". Erected between
1549 and 1577, since 1836 it has housed
the archives of the Crown of Aragon. Immediately adjacent to the Palau Reial

Major looms the watch-tower, the Mirador
del Rei Martí, dating from 1555.
The northern part of the palace was totally
rebuilt in the early 18th century. Today it
is the home of the Museu Frederic Marès,
a "museum of memories", where everything can be found – from kitsch to fine art
– which has been a part of the daily lives
of the Spanish people over the centuries.

The promenade on the Muralla del Mar –
here seen in a photograph taken in 1860 –
used to be one of the city's most popular
meeting places. In the background is the
Castell de Montjuïc, which, like the Ciutadella in the east of the old city, served
both to protect the town and to watch
over it. Whenever land was reclaimed
from the sea, this area was changed; for
example, towards the end of the last century, when the harbour and the Passeig de
Colom were built.

With the industrialization and expansion
of Barcelona, the docks area lost its attraction. It was not until the 1980s that the
city once more turned its face towards the
sea. The docks area was totally transformed; disused warehouses were swept
away, to be replaced by bars and seafood
restaurants. The Moll de la Fusta, designed
by Manuel de Solà-Morales, has developed into what the Passeig de la Muralla once was: a popular and bustling
promenade.

Barcelona is a city not only rich in history, but also bearing the stamp of modernity and of all the rapid changes this involves. Both the city's layout and its individual buildings bear witness to a kind of collective subconscious which, in the course of time, has taken on an architectonic form. The earlier stages in the city's development still followed a traditional pattern: it was a process of adding on, fitting in, and covering over. Hemmed in between the mountains and the sea, the city evolved as a living collage, a huge and colourful patchwork quilt. In the 20th century another feature of Barcelona came to the fore: her intense effort to share in the progress of the modern world.

The architectonic testaments to the city's past include the remains of Romanesque buildings, often below ground or hidden between other structures, as well as splendid Gothic edifices. The old Gothic Llotja, or bourse, has been given a classicist appearance, but the church of Santa Maria del Mar is still preserved as an example of an indigenous Catalan version of the Gothic style. In addition, anyone interested in architectural history will find buildings of the Renaissance and the Baroque.

Barcelona is especially well-known for its many examples of the exuberant architecture of the Modernismo, the Catalan version of Art Nouveau. Many of these masterpieces – whether they are new buildings, extensions or conversions – take the form of an architectural element within an existing ensemble. Even such important cultural edifices as the Teatre del Liceu (the opera house) or the Palau de la Música Catalana (the concert hall) do not stand alone, but rather form a living whole with the neighbouring urban architecture. In what follows, I shall try to trace the development and evolution of the most important testaments to Barcelona's architectural heritage.

During the 16th and 17th centuries, Barcelona seemed to be leading a Sleeping Beauty existence; its population remained stagnant at between 30,000 and 40,000. During the 18th century, however, trade began to flourish and the population increased dramatically, reaching 193,000 by 1857.[1] An important factor in this economic development was the expansion in trade with America, Barcelona thereby benefiting from its maritime location. The rural hinterland of Catalonia supplied it with both people and capital. For a long time structural conditions in the countryside had delayed developments which had changed the face of cities in other parts of Europe a century earlier.

Under Bourbon rule, Catalonia had lost many of her historic rights; her people were moreover forbidden to use their own language in public. The active cultivation of the Catalan language was already on the decline by the end of the 17th century and would not be revived until the end of the 19th century. Paradoxically,

The map shows Barcelona as it was before
industrialization and the expansion of the
city. For military reasons, no building
could be constructed on the plain below
the fortifications. The inner defensive wall,
dating from the 13th century, which followed the course of the Rambla, a dried-
up river bed, separated the prestigious part
of the city from the suburbs with their
monasteries and hospices, and the
slaughterhouses and cultivated fields,
which guaranteed the city's food supply.

Planta de la Ciutat de
Barcelona, Fortalesas, y
Atácos.

...lona.	H....Baluart de Mitjoxn.	P....Portal de Junqueras y Mitja Lluna.	Y.....Moll, y Baluart.
...bal.	I.....Portal de Mar.	Q....Portal del Angel, y Mitja Lluna.	Z.....Sant Bertran.
...lda.	K.....Baluart de Llevant.	R....Portal de St. Sivra.	&....Santa Madrona.
...ana.	L.....Baluart de Sta. Clara.	S....Portal dels Tallers y Mitja Lluna.	El....Atacos.
...de las Pussas.	M....Torre de St. Juan.	T....Portal de St. Antoni.	Nº 1º. Monjuich.
...art de St. Francesch.	N....Portal de St. Daniel.	V....Mitja Lluna de St. Pere.	Nº 2º. Fortalesa sobre St. Bertran.
...on de St. Ramon.	O....Portal nou y Mitja Lluna.	X....Portal de St. Pau.	Barcelona 31 Decembre de 1806.

14

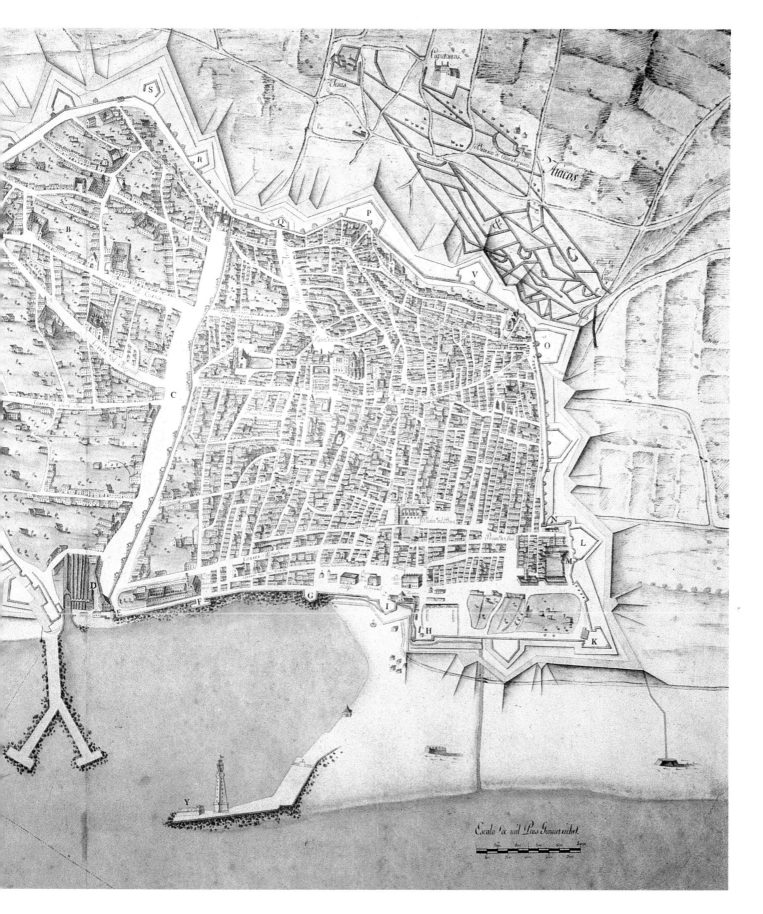

15

it was precisely during this period that economic growth in Catalonia was at its most rapid. During the reign of Charles III, the most enlightened of the Bourbon kings, Barcelona was transformed into a new commercial and artistic centre. In order to expand, the city had to reach out beyond the inner ring formed by the old defensive walls and embrace the suburb of Raval, which was dominated by farms, as well as monasteries, hospices and slaughterhouses until the middle of the 18th century.

From 1720 until 1801, the Military Academy of Mathematics was based in Barcelona, a circumstance of far-reaching importance for the city's building programme. It was from here that most of the Bourbon military engineers graduated and it was they who were charged with the execution of major public construction projects. These included the University of Cervera and Figueres Castle outside Barcelona and, in the city, the Ciutadella militar, Castell de Montjuïc, and a series of barracks. The use of the drawing as the basic teaching aid and architectural textbooks as technical reference works, the gradual introduction of specialization and a division of labour – all these were signs of a modernization in architectural practice whose roots can be traced back to the Military Academy. The military engineers even went so far as to design a whole new quarter: the district of Barceloneta by the sea (1753). It was intended as a residential quarter to house some of the fishermen's and craftsmen's-families who, having been evicted from their homes in the Ribera quarter as a result of the construction of the Citadel (1716–1727), had been crowding into the old quarter or on to the beach. In Barri de la Barceloneta the principles of a new town-planning concept were put into practice: rationality, repetition and hygiene. Characterized by closely spaced rows of houses laid out in straight lines, this neighbourhood came directly from the drawing-board.

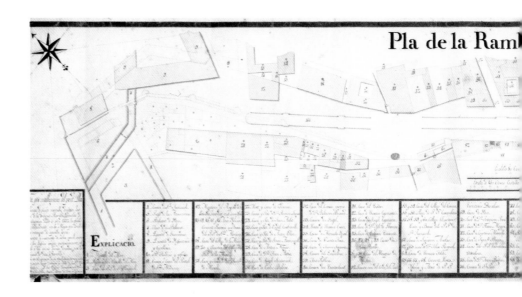

In the course of building the Citadel, 17 per cent of the existing city's buildings were demolished. The architecture of this massive, fortified complex was closely allied to the classicism developed during the 17th century by French military engineers. It served a double purpose typical of complexes of this kind: to protect the city against invasion and, above all, to exercise surveillance over the inhabitants and to nip any rebellion in the bud.

An outstanding figure among the military engineers involved in providing an infrastructure for Catalonia was Jorge Próspero de Verboom, under whose direction the work was carried out. It was he who laid down the general guidelines for the greater part of the military buildings in Catalonia during the first half of the 18th century.[2] However, the work of the engineers was by no means confined to military installations; they also set about shaping the civilian townscape of Barcelona. Thus, for example, they had trees planted along a dry river-bed, and thereby prepared the way for the present-day Ramblas. Likewise they landscaped the terrain which slopes gently down from the Ciutadella and the district of Ribera.

During the 17th and 18th centuries technical advances throughout Europe were indeed decisively influenced by military considerations. It was not until the 19th and 20th centuries that this dominance gave way to other innovative forces; the main impulses for social change now emanated increasingly from trade and industry. Thus it was that for Barcelona too, gradual industrialization became the decisive growth factor in the long term. The traditional craft enterprises were joined by small-scale textile factories, the so-called "talleres de indianas", which, on the South American model, produced printed cotton fabrics. The machines were driven by hand, production being destined for export to America.

LA RAMBLA

"Rambla" means both "promenade" and "gutter", an indication that a river once flowed here from the Tibidabo to the sea. The mid-18th century was a period of steady economic growth in Barcelona. Increased population required the creation of new residential districts. The first building permits on the Rambla's walled side in 1704 foresaw only a partial encroachment of the fortifications, but in 1775 the whole section between the Porta dels Ollers and the Drassanes was razed. The end of the 18th century then witnessed the construction of the generously proportioned promenade, whose central strip, raised higher than the sides, was planted with poplars which provided welcome shade.

Barcelona en lo Añy 1807

LA BARCELONETA

Juan Martín Cermeño, Francisco Paredes,
begun in 1753

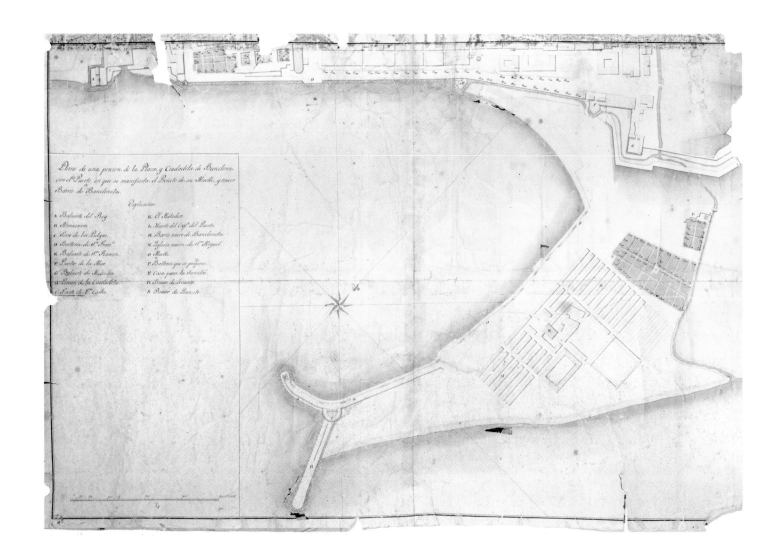

Military engineers led by Juan Martín Cermeño designed and built this quarter outside the ancient city walls next to the beach. It was particularly after the demolition of parts of the Ribera district that small houses were needed to house displaced fishermen and artisans. This was the first district in Barcelona to be created on the drawing-board. Characteristic features were the narrow, parallel streets and the low, block-like buildings, laid out in uniform lines. The two-storeyed buildings contained small two-room flats – each with its own toilet – and measured approximately 35 square metres. This plan heralded the rationalism, homogeneity and geometric structure of the Cerdà plan for the large-scale extension of Barcelona. The uncomplicated structure of the district, and the orientation of the streets towards the Ciutadella were dictated by strategic considerations: from the citadel and the fortress which faced it from Montjuïc, one could observe the whole city. The original plan had only foreseen single-storey houses for Barceloneta, as this was the only way to ensure that ground-floor dwellings received sufficient sunlight. As early as 1839, however, some owners managed to achieve a relaxation of the building regulations, and in 1858 permission was even given for three-storey houses. Finally, in 1886, the city council gave planning consent for a project which included four-storey blocks, albeit on condition that the new streets in question should be at least 10 metres wide.

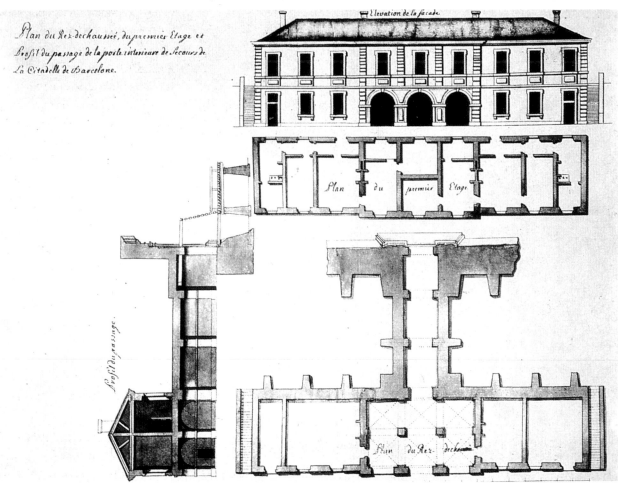

Plan du Rez-de-chaussée, du premier Etage et
Profil du passage de la poste intérieure de Secours de
La Citadelle de Barcelone.

Elevation de la façade.

Plan du premier Etage

Profil du passage

Plan du Rez-de-chaussée

These cotton mills, introduced around 1736, quickly flourished, and made the whole city rich. This growing prosperity expressed itself in the construction of numerous classicist palaces along the major thoroughfares, the construction of new churches in the late Baroque style, and the creation of extensive gardens, for example, the maze of the Marquis of Llupià i Alfarràs in the present-day district of Horta (1793–1804). The same period also saw an increase in population, while Barcelona's workshops spread beyond the city walls. Typical of the times is a building that was remodelled for the Junta de Comercio (or Council of Trade) which was established in 1763. The work was based on designs by Joan Soler i Faneca[3], at the time the city's most highly educated and most modern architect. The building in question is the old Bourse, whose original Gothic structure was transformed and extended in the classicist idiom.

The growth of the city, slowed down by the war with France (1808–1812), gathered pace once more around 1820. In 1830 the first cast-iron columns, imported from England, were erected, followed in 1832 by the installation of the first steam-engine. 1848 saw the construction of the first railway, connecting Barcelona with the town of Mataró and the Maresme coastal region. The quickening pace of industrialization in the 19th century left its mark: by mid-century, Barcelona was already displaying the typical smoke-veiled appearance of a contemporary dynamic European city. The brick and sooty columns of the chimneys – Baudelaire's "obelisks of industry, spewing out their smoky tethers to the firmament" – soon rivalled the towers and belfries of a past age.

Nevertheless, during the first half of the 19th century Barcelona's structure was still that of a fortified mediaeval city. This only changed when, towards the middle of the century, the city council made a determined effort to slough off its constricting corset. The realization of the Eixample – the large scale expansion of Barcelona – represented the most decisive step in the city's history. However, before work began on this great project, the city's ancient centre was subjected to a thorough transformation. In accordance with the classical maxims for a homogeneous, clearly delineated city, streets were straightened, quiet public squares laid out, and prestigious buildings erected. For the short period between 1836 and 1859 the Portal del Mar, giving access to the working-class district of Barceloneta, was the dominant architectural element of the classicist square, Pla del Palau. The ensemble was extended by the residential complex known as the Cases d'En Xifré, designed by Francesc Vila and Josep Buixareu (1836–1840). This period also witnessed the first fruits of Antoni Celles' lessons in architecture (1815–1835) at the Escuela de Llotja in Barcelona. New straight streets such as the Carrer Fernando were defined by façades which shared common elements

LLOTJA

Joan Soler i Faneca, 1764–1794; Joan Fàbregas, Tomàs Soler i Ferrer, 1794–1802
Pla del Palau

In 1764 the Council of Trade decided to restore Barcelona's ancient commodity exchange, which was originally built in 1383.

Soler i Faneca was among the most competent architects of his age. He possessed an extensive library, as well as numerous models exemplifying classical building styles and he was also considered an excellent draughtsman. When he died in 1794, the major part of the work had been completed. The project was then taken over first by Joan Fàbregas, and after his death in 1802, by Joan Soler's son, Tomàs Soler i Ferrer.

Originally the hall, the inner courtyard and the chapel (built somewhat later) were in the Gothic style. Soler i Faneca demolished the dilapidated old church, thus restoring the former unity of the complex. He then placed a classicist building on top of this ensemble, but retained the Gothic structure of the former trading centre. This felicitous adaptation is exemplified by the asymmetrical elevation, the exuberant entrance stairway and the first-floor window pediments. All these harmonious extensions make the Llotja one of the most beautiful, and, in its architectural evolution, one of the most successful buildings in Barcelona. After years of extraneous utilization, among other things as a barracks and a military hospital, it has been used as a stock exchange since 1847.

ARSENAL DE LA CIUTADELLA

Jorge Próspero de Verboom, 1716–1727
Pla del Palau

PLA DEL PALAU

Lithograph by Dumouza y Bichebois,
Paris 1840

The visual axis runs along the Avinguda del Marquès de L'Argentera and the Passeig Isabel II to Montjuïc. The Llotja can be seen in the row of buildings to the right. Opposite it were built, between 1836 and 1840, the Cases d'En Xifré by the classical builders Josep Buixareu and Francesc Vila. These prestigious "apartment blocks", with shops in the ground-storey's arcade, were commissioned by Josep Xifré i Casa, a Catalan "indiano", in other words, someone who had made his fortune in the Americas. Their design was oriented towards the layout of the square, as drawn up by Josep Massanés in 1822. To the left is the old Customs House built by Miquel de Roncali between 1790 and 1792. This handsome square by the sea was, however, only for a few years the central point of the city. As Barcelona expanded towards the Passeig de Gràcia, the Pla del Palau declined in importance and was relegated to the sidelines. From then until very recently, the city turned its back on the sea.

and referred to each other. The secularization laws, allowing the confiscation of Church property from 1835 on, opened up new areas for public building, such as the Plaça Reial, designed by Francesc Daniel Molina i Casamajó (1848–1859), or the Plaça Sant Josep, based on designs by Josep Mas i Vila (1836–1840), which would eventually be the location of the Boqueria market. This transformation of the historic heart of the city reached its climax in 1850. The new Carrer Fernando was now on a level with Pere Blay's Renaissance Palau de la Generalitat, the seat of the Catalan regional government, and with the Gothic Ajuntament. This building, which served as the city hall, also underwent a change at this time (1831–1847). Once again a design by Josep Mas i Vila was used and it was given a late-classicist appearance in order to integrate its appearance with the new Plaça de Sant Jaume. Since then, this has been the administrative and political heart of the city.

Bursting at the seams, it would have made sense for Barcelona to expand on the empty spaces outside the city walls. Since military regulations prohibited any building here, however, important buildings continued to be constructed in the ancient city centre. For example, the Teatre del Liceu, the opera house, was squeezed into a corner of the Rambles; and while Elies Rogent's University (1859–1873) was built on the boundary to the Eixample, its main façade faced the old town and its back was turned on the projected new city. Even the Palau de la Música (1905–1908), that beacon of Catalan national pride in the style of Modernismo, was put up on a plot tucked away among poky and unprepossessing old-town alleyways.[4]

In order to keep the expansion of the city beyond the walls under control, the central government in Madrid promulgated the expansion plan put forward by the engineer Ildefons Cerdà in 1859. Barcelona's councillors were not, however, disposed to having the development of their city laid down from on high, and proceeded to announce a competition of their own, which attracted all of Barcelona's most able and respected architects. The winner was Antoni Rovira i Trias, who, along with Miquel Garriga i Roca, was considered to be a specialist in town planning and highly sensitive to its various requirements. Rovira proposed a city based on concentric circles with radial "spokes". The central government under Isabella II, however, insisted on a plan which proved to be far more modern and incomparably more adaptable to later developments, namely the Eixample project put forward by Cerdà. The people of Barcelona did not find it easy to accept a plan which was neither of their own making nor in accordance with their own ideas, and, to cap it all, had been imposed on them by Madrid. Since then the city has seen very different theoretical approaches to town plan-

PISSOIRS

Miquel Garriga i Roca, 1848–1856

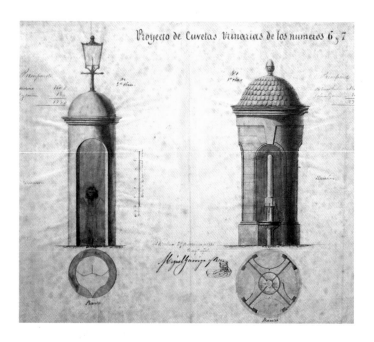

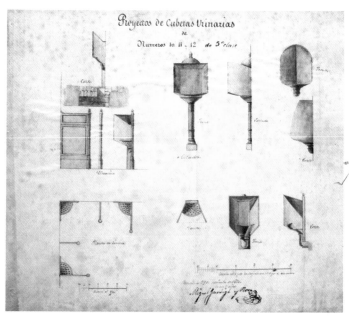

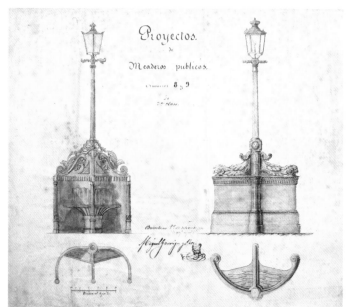

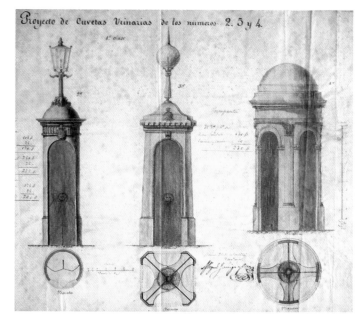

The early decades of the 19th century witnessed an outburst of luxurious "street furniture" aiming at a standard of comfort which could match the interiors of the houses of the bourgeoisie. Streetlamps, benches, fountains, kiosks and pissoirs were installed, and from then on made a decisive contribution to the outward appearance of the city.

ning issues, appearing alongside one another: the centralizing plan put forward by Rovira and Garriga, the repetitive homogeneity of Cerdà, the monumentality of Jaussely, and the rationalism of the group of architects known as GATCPAC (Grupo de Artístas y Técnicos Catalanes para el Progreso de la Arquitectura Contemporánea).[5]

Ildefons Cerdà proposed an isotropic, almost endless layout, which shifted the centre of the city to the Plaça de les Glòries and filled up the space intended for development with a uniform pattern of building. The core of his design was a module consisting of a city block, square in shape and generous in its proportions (113.33 x 113.33 metres), whose corners were – somewhat surprisingly – truncated to produce 45° angles. The motive behind this latter touch was to make it easier for trains to turn the corners; Cerdà imagined that the city would soon be criss-crossed by railway lines from one side to the other. This vision never materialized, but the regular sequence of intersections, thus shaped, still remains.

The realization of Cerdà's project was a key moment in the development of modern Barcelona. The urban texture, in all its variety and disorder, was now absorbed into a coherent plan, thus becoming part of a whole. Barcelona not only owes its expansion to Cerdà, but also its totally new overall appearance. The formal structural elements of Cerdà's city blocks represent a basic pattern ubiquitous in modern Barcelona. The flexibility of their design permitted a measure of variety, ranging from terraced housing to detached public buildings. The novel Modernismo buildings were provided with an appropriate background by the uniform appearance of the blocks, against which they could unfold their stylistic individuality. In terms of traffic, Cerdà's plan also proved appropriate: the extraordinary capacity of his street network has managed for over a century to absorb the constantly growing volume of traffic without difficulty.[6]

Following double page:

The former Jaumandreu textile works in the Poble Nou district (above left; photograph taken around 1900); Barcelona's oldest railway station, the Estació de França, with the engine that operated the shuttle service between Barcelona and Mataró from 1848 (below right); a brickworks, since demolished (above right); Les Drassanes (below right).

LES DRASSANES
Plaça del Portal de la Pau

This shipyard is one of the best-preserved and most beautiful in the whole Mediterranean area. The original complex was built between 1284 and 1348, but was already enlarged in the 1370s and 80s. Each of the eight sheds could accommodate one ship. Plans dating from 1390 foresaw further extensions that provided for the construction of up to thirty galleys concurrently. In 1714, the military moved into the Drassanes, and from then on the buildings served a great variety of functions: barracks, military hospital, vehicle workshop. Today the sheds are used by the Museu Maritím. Among the outstanding exhibits is a facsimile of the Royal Galley from the fleet which helped the Spaniards to their decisive victory over the Ottoman Turks at Lepanto.

L'EIXAMPLE

Ildefons Cerdà i Suñer, 1859

The plan drawn up by road, canal and dockbuilding engineer Ildefons Cerdà is based on a regular, rectangular grid. The square-shaped residential areas were to have open, perimeter block construction, reaching no higher than four storeys and including extensive green areas. None of the streets was less than 20 metres wide, some 30 metres, and some as much as 50 metres. The truncated corners of the blocks gave rise to a small square at each intersection. A purpose of these truncations was to make it easier for the "mobile steam-engines", which Cerdà thought would soon be traversing the city, to get round the corners. Cerdà's proposals for the Barcelona of the future constituted a clear response to the cramped and highly unsanitary living conditions in of the old city.

The original plan for an open style of construction, with generally no more than two rows of buildings per block, was based on a projected population density of 250 persons per hectare and could not be realized. By 1890, there were 1400 per hectare, and by 1925 already 2000. The blocks were enclosed on all four sides, the buildings themselves were made higher and deeper, and finally the inner courtyards were privatized.

PLANO DE LOS ALREDEDORES DE LA CIUDAD DE BARCELONA Y PROYECTO DE SU REFORMA Y ENSANCHE

S. ANDRES DE PALOMAR

CEMENTERIO

GRAN BOSQUE

LEYENDA DEL PROYECTO

MEDITERRÁNEO

TEATRE DEL LICEU

Miquel Garriga i Roca, 1845–1847; Josep
Oriol Mestres i Esplugas, 1862 and 1874
La Rambla 61–65

Oddly enough, the initiative for Barcelona's first opera house came from army officers billeted in the convent of Montsió. On the pretext of outfitting the troops, they collected money to build a theatre in their neighbourhood. However, the nuns successfully demanded their convent back. As a result, a new site had to be sought, and one was eventually found on the Rambla in 1844. Anyone who contributed to a kind of co-operative fund to finance the project received the rights to a seat or a box. Thus the Teatre del Liceu was built within three years, under the direction of Garriga i Roca and his assistant Mestres i Esplugas. More than 4000 guests attended its inauguration.

The auditorium was based on that of La Scala in Milan, albeit somewhat larger, and also somewhat larger than the famous opera houses in Paris, Lisbon and Madrid. It burned down in 1861, but managed to reopen a year later. Mestres based his reconstruction meticulously on the original plans, with the exception of two tiers of boxes which were not rebuilt.

The photograph shows the main façade as rebuilt by Mestres in 1874. His solution elicited vehement criticism from his fellow architects at the time. His design was written off as mediocre, too French in its inspiration, and out of place in its context.

TEATRE DEL LICEU

Auditorium; plan of the extensions by Ignasi de Solà-Morales

In 1883 the stage and auditorium were completely remodelled by Pere Falqués. At the same time, the boxes were given an extravagant neo-Baroque decor. The Liceu is currently being remodelled once more by Ignasi de Solà-Morales, the incorporation of neighbouring plots of land allowing for considerable enlargement.

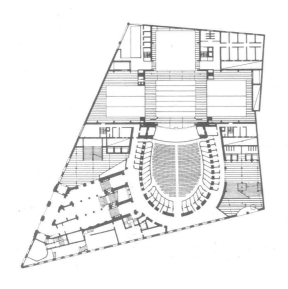

PLAÇA REIAL

Francesc Daniel Molina i Casamajó,
1848–1859

This elegant 19th-century square was made possible by the secularization of church property. Generously proportioned, it occupies the site of a former Capuchin monastery, and evinces a clearly ordered structure: the inner courtyard, measuring 56 by 84 metres, is enclosed by classical façades, only one side being open to the Rambla. Appropriate lighting is provided by lamps added later by the young Antoni Gaudí. Once thought of as a sub-tropical garden and oasis of repose, the square had a raised fountain added to it in 1878, surrounded by palms and flower-beds. However, this salon-like piazza soon developed into a much-frequented, noisy and hectic site. The secularization of a monastery also gave rise to the Plaça del Duc de Medinaceli on the Passeig de Colom, with its column honouring Admiral Galceran Marquet.

PLAÇA DEL DUC DE MEDINACELI
Francesc Daniel Molina i Casamajó, 1849

THE BEGINNINGS OF MODERNISMO AT THE TIME OF THE 1888 WORLD EXHIBITION

In 1885 an international corporation specializing in prefabricated components for exhibition buildings succeeded in winning over the Mayor of Barcelona, Señor Rius i Taulet, to the idea of an Exposició Universal. The foremost advocate of the project within the city administration was a former Galician military officer named Eugenio Serrano de Casanova. He had been fascinated by his visits to the World Exhibitions of Paris, Vienna and Antwerp and now wanted to create the framework for an equally spectacular event in Spain. Serrano requested a 20-hectare plot and was allocated the wasteland around the citadel. However, it soon transpired that Serrano's designs were of a very poor technical quality. Some of the already completed buildings required reinforcement, and even this did not save a number from collapse. Finally, responsibility for the construction work was transferred to an architect, Elies Rogent.

Some of the buildings on the exhibition site in the Parc de la Ciutadella had, however, been completed long before, for example, the cascade fountain and the Umbracle. Most of the buildings subsequently added were temporary structures, which were demolished once the Exhibition was over. Among the few to have been preserved are the Café-Restaurant del Parc, which was, however, never a catering establishment. It was indeed designed with such a purpose in mind, but it was not completed in time. Today it houses the Zoological Museum.

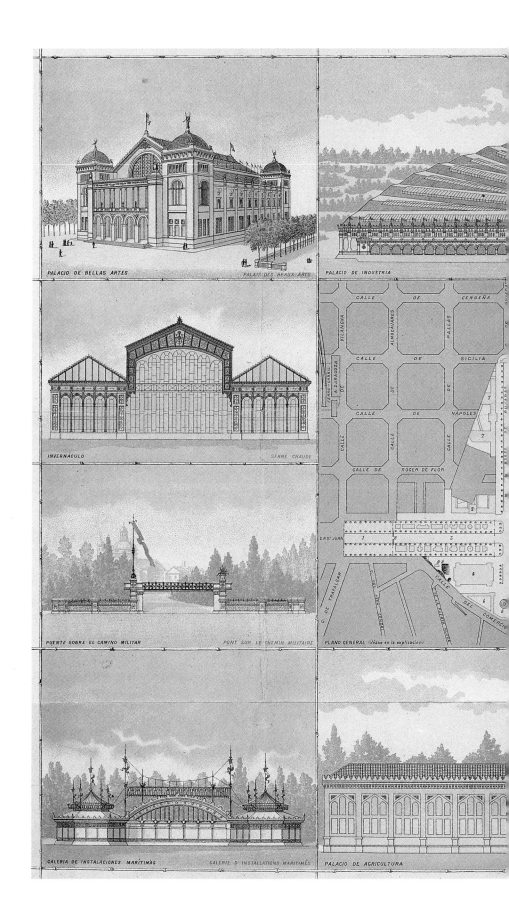

PALACIO DE BELLAS ARTES   PALAIS DES BEAUX ARTS   PALACIO DE INDUSTRIA

INVERNÁCULO   SERRE CHAUDE

PUENTE SOBRE EL CAMINO MILITAR   PONT SUR LE CHEMIN MILITAIRE   PLANO GENERAL (Véase en la explicación)

GALERIA DE INSTALACIONES MARÍTIMAS   GALERIE D'INSTALLATIONS MARITIMES   PALACIO DE AGRICULTURA

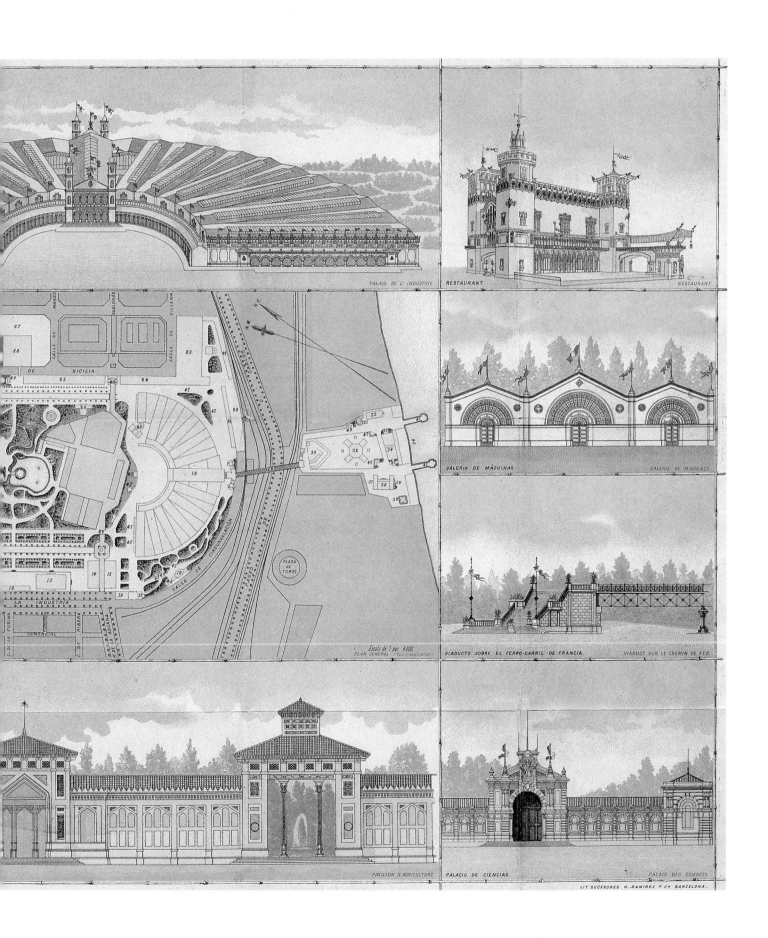

PALAIS DE L'INDUSTRIE   RESTAURANT   RESTAURANT

GALERIA DE MÁQUINAS   GALERIE DE MACHINES

VIADUCTO SOBRE EL FERRO-CARRIL DE FRANCIA   VIADUCT SUR LE CHEMIN DE FER

Escala de 1 por 4.000
PLAN GENERAL (Voir l'explication)

PAVILLON D'AGRICULTURE   PALACIO DE CIENCIAS   PALAIS DES SCIENCES

LIT. SUCESORES N. RAMIREZ Y Cª BARCELONA.

ARC DEL TRIOMF

Josep Vilaseca i Casanovas, 1888
Passeig de Lluís Companys

There is a touch of the oriental about the
Arc del Triomf, in particular the columns
and the round arches with the coats of
arms of the Spanish provinces. By contrast, the complex brick ornamentation
and the tops of the columns are more reminiscent of mediaeval motifs. Presumably
Vilaseca, like many of his colleagues at
the Exposició Universal, was seeking to
draw attention to Spain's Islamic heyday.
This triumphal arch was conceived as the
gateway to the Exhibition: behind it, a
magnificent square, flanked by trees,
lamps and bronze statues, leads to Lluís
Domènech i Montaner's Café-Restaurant
del Parc.
On both sides above the passage through
the arch there is a frieze. The theme of
one is the participation of Madrid, as repre-
senting the central authority of Spain, in
Barcelona's World Exhibition, while the
other expresses the city's gratitude to the
nations represented. In actual fact a
proud, 210-metre high tower designed by
Eugenio Serrano should have been the
symbol of the Exhibition, visible from far
and wide, but this project was never realized. The Arc del Triomf would never
enjoy the popularity and international
fame of other World Exhibition structures,
for example, the 1889 Eiffel Tower in Paris.

CAFE-RESTAURANT DEL PARC

Lluís Domènech i Montaner, 1887–1888
Passeig de Pujades / Parc de la Ciutadella

CASCADE Y FOUNTAIN

Josep Fontserè i Mestres, Antoni Gaudí
i Cornet, 1875–1881
Parc de la Ciutadella

WATER-TOWER

Josep Fontserè i Mestres, Antoni Gaudí
i Cornet, 1874–1877; Lluís Clotet i Ballús,
Ignacio Paricio Ansuategui, 1986–1989
Carrer de Wellington 48

Years before, and independently of, the
World Exhibition, the fountains and the
little lake in the Parc de la Ciutadella had
already been laid out. The picturesque
complex with its decorative sculpture was,
however, not without its critics. Josep Fontserè was accused of merely copying Espe-
randieu's French neo-Baroque, as exemplified in a similar project in Marseilles.
Today's debate, however, concerns the extent to which the influence of Antoni
Gaudí can already be discerned: he had
been involved in the project as an architectural student.

There is certainly no doubt at all concern-
ing Gaudí's involvement in the water-
tower, which is situated close to the fountain on the Carrer de Wellington. A
gridded brick structure, that fits tightly into
the square-shaped building, supports a
large water-tank on the roof. The water-
pressure for the fountains is provided by
this tank. Gaudí's technical calculations
for the structure so impressed the Professor
of Statics at Barcelona's Architectural College, that he recognized them as equiva-
lent to an examination pass in this subject
and exempted him from the otherwise obligatory lectures. Quite rightly, it would
seem, for the building is still standing.
Since its restoration and enlargement by
Lluís Clotet and Ignacio Paricio Ansuategui, it is now used by the city for exhibitions.

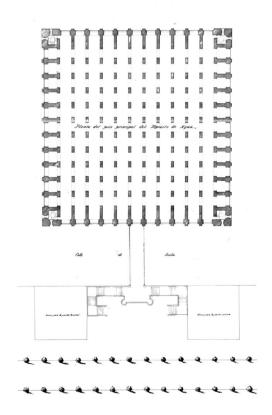

UMBRACLE

Josep Fontserè i Mestres, 1883–1884;
Jaume Gustà i Bondia, 1886; Josep Amargós
i Samaranch, 1888
Parc de la Ciutadella

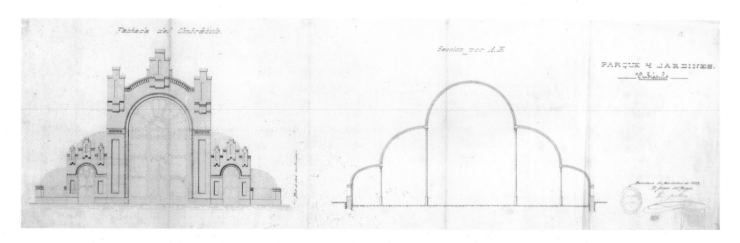

PASSEIG DE GRACIA, 1888

The Passeig de Gràcia was at that time the
connecting thoroughfare between the old
city and the suburb of Gràcia, which was
incorporated into the Barcelona munici-
pality – incidentally, against the wishes of
its inhabitants – in 1897. As soon as the
shops closed to make way for leisure activities, the street became a favourite promenade of the bourgeoisie. Every Sunday the
Clavé choirs sang here, and people would
meet for a glass of wine or cup of choco-
late. At the Criadero, the Tivoli and the
Euterpe there was dancing, or else one
could decide to patronize one of the
numerous theatres. In the Campos Eliseos
park there were opportunities to row on
the lake or ride on a roundabout.
Around the turn of the century, building
became more concentrated, and there
were exclusive shops and elegant cafés to
attract a prosperous clientèle. Thus the
Passeig de Gràcia developed into one of
Europe's most attractive boulevards.

The Plaça de Catalunya, then as now an important traffic intersection, links the old city and the Ramblas with the Passeig de Gràcia, the Rambla de Catalunya and the heart of the Eixample. During the World Exhibition, it was the site of a variety of attractions which fascinated Catalans, Spaniards and foreign visitors alike. There was a Waterloo Panorama, a horse circus, an aviary, and much else besides. The whole ensemble was a purely temporary exhibition structure.

Barcelona's 19th-century expansion reached its peak in the 1888 World Exhibition, after enjoying a period of economic boom, the "febre d'or" ("gold fever") from 1875 to 1884. This was followed by the 1884/85 crisis, caused by the free-trade policies of the government in Madrid. By the time of the Exhibition, the city was already pushing out along the Passeig de Gràcia and the Rambla de Catalunya, thus utilizing that part of the Eixample terrain nearest both the Gran Via and the historic city centre.[7]

The appearance that the city took on after its expansion and development during the first phase of the Cerdà plan was still far removed from that of present-day Barcelona. Infrastructure measures took precedence over actual building. The streets were marked out, the sidewalks could be used and street lamps had been installed, but at this early stage the building density was still quite low. Most of the sites still consisted either entirely of wasteland or else housed temporary structures such as storage sheds and the like.[8] Typical were houses of four storeys, the ground floor being occupied by workshops.[9] The many open spaces were often transformed into extensive gardens by the well-to-do.

Among the architects of this first Eixample phase were Josep Oriol Mestres, Josep Vilaseca, Jeroni Granell, August Font, Joan Martorell, Josep Fontserè and Enric Sagnier i Villavecchia, who are generally regarded as the forerunners of Modernismo. Their eclectic designs follow classical models of composition, rich in ornamentation and historical references.

The early nineties saw a further, important progress in the plan's development. Revised planning regulations in 1891 allowed for higher buildings. The ground floors came to be occupied by the sorts of shops characteristic of Modernismo: pharmacies, bakeries, pâtisseries, general stores – which all contributed a further typical note to the Barcelona of the Age of Industry. Some of the low, simple buildings of the early Eixample phase were replaced with more extravagant structures which increasingly bore the hallmarks of the architects of Modernismo.

The World Exhibition of 1888 took place on the Ciutadella site, confirming the municipal takeover of erstwhile military land. The most important buildings, such as the Governor's Palace, the Arsenal and the Chapel, were preserved. The existing layout of Josep Fontserè's Park was utilized and adapted for the building of the Pavilion.

Many months before the opening of the Exhibition, the Columbus Column was erected on the spot where the Rambla de Santa Mònica meets the sea. The scaffolding took the form of an impressive metal structure designed by Joan Torras. Alongside the Triumphal Arch and the Umbracle – a palm house with a

54

slat roof which let in air while providing shade – is Lluís Domènech i Montaner's well-known restaurant building, popularly christened the Castell dels Tres Dragons (Castle of the Three Dragons) which is still the symbol of the Exhibition. This building is a clear sign of the progress achieved in Catalan architecture. It appears in a playful, historic style, bearing witness to the regained heights of the craftsmen's skills, be they potters, metalworkers, plasterers, joiners or masons.

Modernismo was without any doubt the result of the industrialization of Catalonia, but at the same time it also allowed specific traits of the region to flourish. It represented a comprehensive movement, taking in crafts and decorative arts in all their variety. Support for this development came from such centres of craft training as the Taller de Industrias Artísticas – a workshop and school for craftsmen which was later housed in the Castle of the Three Dragons mentioned above –, the Centro de Artes Decorativas, and the Taller de Oficios Tradicionales.

The artistry evident in the massive brick walls of the Café-Restaurant, along with the impressive partitioning of the spacious interior by means of metal structures, allow a comparison of this architecture with a work as unique and proto-rationalist as Hendrick Petrus Berlage's Bourse in Amsterdam, built between 1897 and 1903.

Although the Exhibition took place in the Modernismo era and included architecture of a high quality, it had barely any influence on Barcelona's urban landscape. True, it served to reshape the site of the ancient Citadel and to integrate it with the Eixample, but whereas the Exhibition was based in the extreme east of Barcelona, the city was expanding in precisely the opposite direction, namely westwards. In so doing, it followed the axis of the Passeig de Gràcia, which had already become the showpiece centre of the city, a broad thoroughfare with impressive buildings, a place where the bourgeoisie went to stroll, to see and be seen.[10] It was here that the Barcelona of the well-to-do was on display, a middle-class which had found a suitable stage on which to present itself in the World Exhibition and in the prestige edifices of Modernismo. At the same time, however, a working-class city was also emerging. It was growing up on the outskirts, and in the extensive industrial district behind the Ciutadella and the Estació de França, the nearby railway station. The district which was taking shape here, Poble Nou, came to be known as the "Manchester of Catalonia".

Working-class housing estates were built in areas close to the great mid-19th century factories, such as the Vapor Vell in the Sants district, the Batlló and Folch factories, and the España Industrial and Maquinista Terrestre y Marítima works.

UNIVERSITY

Elies Rogent Amat, 1859–1873
Plaça de la Universitat

The University of Barcelona was the most magnificent building to be designed by Rogent, the great harbinger and mentor of Catalan Modernismo. The plan of the main building, 130 metres long by 83 wide, followed the classical models of symmetry and axial alignment. Its stylistic sources range from Romanesque motifs to German Classicism, with quotations from Byzantine architecture and, most particularly, the early Italian Renaissance. It was Rogent who introduced the ideas of French Rationalism, derived for instance from Viollet-le-Duc, to Catalan architecture, thus entailing a retreat from academic stylistic purity and a positive understanding of the freedom of eclecticism. On the occasion of the Industrial Exhibition of 1877, two fragments of bridges were set up in front of the main façade as plinths for the display of outstanding technical achievements. The photograph shows the locomotive which ran on the railway line between Barcelona and Mataró.

This company was founded in Barcelona in 1855. It started in a few workshops on the Carrer dels Tallers and the Carrer de Sant Pau, which were followed shortly afterwards by a first factory in Barceloneta, a few sections of which are still extant. Between 1918 and 1925 the factory, depicted above, was built in the district of Sant Andreu. The First World War had given an enormous impetus to the Catalan steel industry, and "La Maquinista" was able to expand its production of railway engines. The building erected in Sant Andreu is based on a sequence of halls identical in appearance but put to different uses: warehouses and workshops for making steam-boilers and mechanical parts and for assembly and adjustment. The columns and roof consist of riveted iron plates, the same form of construction used for the Eiffel Tower in Paris. Although the whole building consists of one single metal structure, the outward appearance of the façade is, ironically enough, highly traditional – the brick cladding, pilasters, gables and cornices being altogether typical of factory buildings of the time.

BATLLO FACTORY

Rafael Guastavino i Moreno, 1870–1875;
Joan Rubió i Bellvé, 1927–1931;
Manuel Baldrich, 1961 and 1966
Carrer del Comte d'Urgell 173–221

The Batlló factory was one of the largest textile works in Barcelona, taking up four of Cerdà's quadrangular blocks. The complex was designed between 1868 and 1869 by Rafael Guastavino; it later became known as the "Vapor Batlló", on account of its slender octagonal chimney which acted as the outlet for a steam-engine inside. The factory closed down in 1895, production being transferred to a site outside Barcelona, on account of the frequent disturbances arising from the social tensions in the city itself. In 1906 the site was acquired by the "Mancomunidad de Catalunya", the first organ of Catalan self-government. Four years later it built the College of Economics here; the building is still used for higher education today. When it was converted for use as part of the University, the existing industrial structure was altered and two wings added to house lecture-rooms. The conversions carried out to the main building and to the chapel entrance by Joan Rubió i Bellvé in the late 1920s are worthy of special mention. The most recent extensions are the work of Manuel Baldrich.

HIDROELECTRICA DE CATALUNYA

Pere Falqués i Urpi, 1896–1897; Telm
Fernàndez, 1910; J. M. Sanz, A. Torra,
P. Fochs, 1977–1980
Avinguda de Vilanova 12

Following the World Exhibition of 1888, the "Central Catalana de Electricidad", then responsible for Catalonia's electricity supply, commissioned Pere Falqués to build a new power station, which was finally completed in 1897. The building consists of two large, parallel halls accommodating the turbines and steam generators. Above the turbine room is a storey housing the accumulators, while the two basements contain the service and control rooms. The riveted metal construction absorbs the vibrations caused by the steam-engine, while the load-bearing element is of coarse brickwork. This explains why the external appearance of the building is based on a curious symbiosis of masonry and iron. The original design provided for bronze reliefs to decorate the façade, which was to be surmounted by two large pyramids. These were, however, never built. In the late 1970s the whole complex was renovated and now houses the administrative offices of the present-day Catalan power supply company, "Hidroeléctrica de Catalunya".

STREET LAMP

Pere Falqués i Urpi
Passeig de Lluís Companys

The incipient social conflicts led to a situation in which – precisely at the time of the Exhibition, when Barcelona was celebrating her industrial production – most of the major businesses were locating their factories outside the metropolis, along the Llobregat, Ter and Cardener rivers. In this, the businesses were belatedly following the 18th-century British model of paternalistic industrial estates.[11]

Just as industrialization provided the driving force behind Modernismo, so architecture needed a generation of pre-modern masters such as Elies Rogent, Joan Torras i Guardiola and Rafael Guastavino i Moreno, who paved the way for the new style with their theories and their own designs. Joan Torras specialized in the calculation, drawing and construction of the new metal structures.[12] Guastavino, who came from Valencia, created such grandiose buildings during his period in Barcelona as the Batlló factory on the Carrer del Comte d'Urgell (1870–1875) or the Asland works (1901–1904). In fact it was Guastavino who perfected the construction of the traditional Catalan brick vault, a structure of exceptional lightness, by introducing iron tension rods to make possible the enormous domes needed to roof his very large interiors. In 1881 he went to the United States, where he created such buildings as Grand Central Station and Queensboro Bridge Market Hall in New York, Boston Library, and a number of churches.

This new construction principle rendered massive supporting piers superfluous, and thus relieved traditional brick structures of their heavy appearance. The iron tension rods could either be exposed to view or hidden behind the walls. The idea was to combine brickwork and iron in such a way that the brick structure of the walls and ceilings takes the pressure, while the iron tension rods serve to counteract the shearing forces. Both brick domes and iron trusses had long been part of the inventory of Catalan architects; what was new was the combination of the two. The guiding criterion in this innovation was Viollet-le-Duc's formal concept of structure, in which the distribution of forces was given a totally new interpretation, based on the separation of skeleton and skin.[13] It was thus only to be expected that this system should become one of the bases of modern Catalan architecture. A pioneering example was Elies Rogent's Almacenes Generales de Comercio (1874), the dock warehouse complex, which has unfortunately fallen victim to the recently constructed Olympic Village.

Elies Rogent, the first director of the Escuela de Arquitectura, founded in Barcelona in 1877, was the actual mentor and harbinger of the modernistic architects.[14] His project for Barcelona University, mentioned above, is strongly imbued with the spirit of Viollet-le-Duc, while also betraying the influence of such architects as Leo von Klenze and Friedrich von Gärtner.

Shops beneath the arcades of the Carrer del Rec; stall for the sale of fresh meat from fighting bulls at the Ninot market.

MERCAT DE SANT JOSEP

Josep Mas i Vila, 1836–1840
La Rambla 85–89

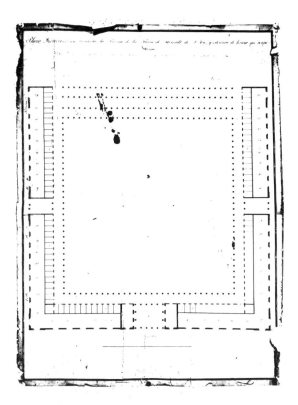

When the Pla de la Boqueria grew too
small for the number of traders wishing to
use it, and the stalls began to flow out on
to the Rambla de Sant Josep, leading to
considerable obstruction, the city council
decided to act. The site of the burnt-out
Carmelite convent on the Plaça de Sant
Josep was selected for a new large-scale
market-place; it was to take the form of an
open-air courtyard framed by an Ionic arcade. But even before building work was
finished, the first voices were raised in protest, both from those living nearby and
from the traders themselves. Both groups
clamoured for a covered market hall, and
in 1870 they got their way.

MERCAT DEL BORN

Josep Fontserè i Mestres, Josep Maria Cornet
i Mas, 1873–1876
Plaça Comercial 12

It was the new covered markets, the Mercat del Born in particular, that ushered in the "Iron Age" of Spanish architecture. Barcelona could point proudly to the fact that all the necessary materials came from Catalonia. Covered by an octagonal domed roof the main building is made up of two naves of different lengths which intersect at its centre. Because smaller aisles run parallel to this long hall, the building as a whole has a rectangular form.

The Mercat de Sant Antoni building, which takes up the whole of one of Cerdà's quadrangles, is the only covered market in Barcelona to keep to his specifications. Two diagonal naves form a St Andrew's cross, their clear geometric structure corresponding precisely to the design which Cerdà envisaged for public squares. On weekdays, exotic fruits, fresh vegetables and fish are on sale here, while on Sundays the second-hand booksellers set up their stalls on the Ronda de Sant Antoni.

MERCAT DE SANT ANTONI

Antoni Rovira i Trias, Josep Maria Cornet i Mas, 1876–1882
Carrer del Comte d'Urgell

Probably the most spectacular achievements of the advances in technology were the new covered markets, such as the already mentioned Mercat de Sant Josep, along with the Mercat del Born (1873–1876) and the Mercat de Sant Antoni (1876–1882). The Santa Caterina market, made entirely of wood, had appeared as early as 1847 – hitherto, since the Middle Ages, markets had been held in squares in the open. By the second half of the 19th century, however, the trend was increasingly towards covered markets. The new technology of cast-iron columns and metal buttresses could be used to good advantage in covering large areas. The market as the hub of daily activity, with its abundant variety of produce, the brilliance of its colours, the enticing allures of its aromas and the delightful hubbub of voices, has remained the hallmark and the rendezvous of Barcelona's various neighbourhoods to this day.

As early as the 1888 World Exhibition the prototypes of Modernismo were to be seen in eye-catching positions around the city, among them the apartment blocks and two publishing houses (since altered) designed by a pupil of Elies Rogent, Lluís Domènech i Montaner. The former Montaner i Simon publishing house (1879–1885) is a prime example of the pre-modernist, proto-rationalist style. Today the home of the Fundació Antoni Tàpies, its façade is surmounted by a unique and curious sculpture going by the name of "Nube y Silla" (Cloud and Chair). The Thomas publishing house (1895–1898) is now the headquarters of another publisher, B. D. Ediciones de Diseño, an active patron of innovative, post-modern design.

Lluís Domènech i Montaner's two most complex works are the Palau de la Música Catalana (1905–1908), and the Hospital de la Santa Creu i de Sant Pau (1902–1911). The former, while basically proto-rationalist in its spatial division, enjoys an ornamentation so exuberant as to be almost ecstatic; while the latter is almost a city in itself, the influence of the "Beaux Arts" unmistakable in its design. The whole of Domènech's work is outstanding testimony to how architecture, in collaboration with craftsmanship, can integrate a whole variety of applied arts into a harmonious whole. The moving force was a desire for an artistic synthesis, which runs as a central theme through the architecture of William Morris, Walter Gropius, and Le Corbusier, right through to the Mexican syncretists of the 1940s.

Lluís Domènech i Montaner had already hinted at the first signs of the approaching Modernismo in his *En busca de una arquitectura nacional (The Search for a National Architecture)*, published in 1878.[15] The same period saw the earliest works of Antoni Gaudí i Cornet, who had had the benefit of an academic training, and had passed through the Beaux Arts school. In addition, he evinced great

MONTANER I SIMON PUBLISHING HOUSE

Lluís Domènech i Montaner, 1879–1885;
Lluís Domènech i Girbau and Roser Amadó
i Cercós, 1985–1990
Carrer d'Aragó 255

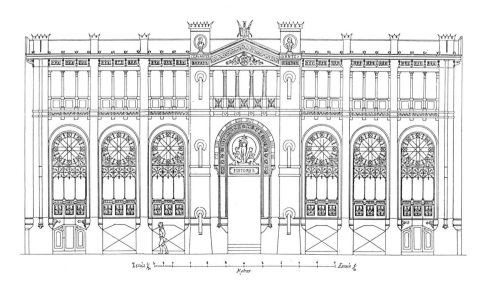

MONTANER I SIMON PUBLISHING HOUSE

Rooms as they appear following the building's conversion into the Fundació Antoni Tàpies; plans

Domènech's signature is clearly apparent, both in the limpid structure of this former publishing house and in the effects produced by the cast-iron construction. Today the building houses the foundation set up by the Catalan painter Antoni Tàpies; the device on the roof is his airy sculpture "Cloud and Chair", consisting of two-and-a-half kilometres of aluminium wire. Apart from this, the façade maintains its original appearance, the relief above the entrance quoting the rediscovered Moorish style of ornamentation.

The interior of the building was refashioned with great sensitivity as a forum for modern art by Roser Amadó and Lluís Domènech, a great-grandson of the architect. The space-structuring columns and galleries were preserved and skilfully complemented by very reticent exhibition fittings. The tall, solid wooden bookshelves belonging to the publishing house now stand in the Foundation library.

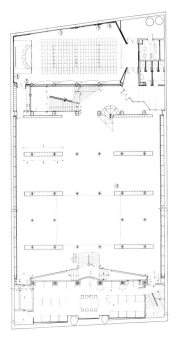

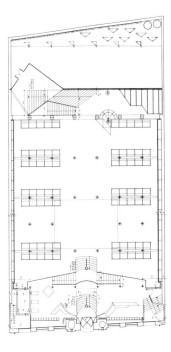

CASA THOMAS

Lluís Domènech i Montaner, 1895–1898;
Francesc Guàrdia i Vial, 1912; Studio PER,
1979
Carrer de Mallorca 291–293

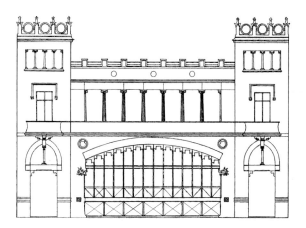

The Casa Thomas was originally a two-storeyed residential and commercial building. When the building was substantially enlarged in 1912, the ground floor was preserved and three completely new residential storeys were built on top of it. What had originally been the first floor was reconstructed as the fourth. After careful restoration work in the late 1970s, the ground floor is now used as a showroom for modern design.

CASA MARTI

Josep Puig i Cadafalch, 1895–1896
Carrer de Montsió 3

Based on a neo-Gothic concept in its structure and ornamentation, the Casa Martí
combines both modernistic and historicis-
ing elements.
"Els Quatre Gats" (The Four Cats), on the
ground floor of Casa Martí, has always
been a popular meeting-place for artists. It
was fitted out by the painter Pere Romeu,
who wanted somewhere to match up to
"Le Chat Noir" in Paris. Pablo Picasso was
one of the regulars.

FINCA GÜELL

Antoni Gaudí i Cornet, 1884–1887
Avinguda de Pedralbes 77

admiration for the structural rationalism of Viollet-le-Duc and the mediaeval ethic of John Ruskin.

Gaudí, who at first worked together with Josep Fontserè, started his architectural career with the Casa Vicens (1878–1888) in Gràcia, a suburban villa displaying mediaeval and Islamic influences, commissioned by Manuel Vicens i Montaner. It was followed by the Convento Teresiano (1880–1890), whose interior is reminiscent of the Mudéjar style; the Casa Calvet (1889–1904) in the Carrer de Casp, and finally in this first phase, the Palau Güell (1885–1890), in the immediate vicinity of the Ramblas, whose splendid interior decoration, with its suggestions of the Middle Ages, is exactly oriented towards the rays of the sun as they shine in. In this first creative phase, Gaudí started out from a position in which eclecticism predominated, before tending more towards neo-Gothicism, while all the time showing the first signs of sympathy with Charles Rennie Mackintosh and Art Nouveau.

CASA VICENS

Antoni Gaudí i Cornet, 1876–1888
Carrer de les Carolines 18–24

At the age of 26, shortly after completing his architectural studies, Gaudí was privately commissioned to build a summer residence for the family of the brick and ceramics manufacturer Manuel Vicens, one of his early patrons. At his disposal he had a relatively small plot of land in Gràcia, which at the time was beyond the city limits. In spite of the small area available, he succeeded in creating a spacious park, a result he achieved by placing the house not in the centre, but at one edge of the rectangular site. Subsequent enlargements led to the destruction of parts of the garden, but the artistic fence facing the street, with its cast-iron dwarf-palm fronds, has been preserved.

The building itself is a *Gesamtkunstwerk* (total work of art). While the ground floor façades are still if anything in the Spanish style, Gaudí used the upper storeys and the roof to conjure up increasingly Moorish impressions. The dominant features are the chequered tiled surfaces and the banded turrets, bay windows and gables. The bricks and tiles came, naturally enough, from the client's own factory – who thus had, in addition to a summer home, a showroom for his products.

The playful design of the house and garden, along with the opulent decoration of the façades, are reminiscent of Oriental palaces and make the building seem larger than it really is.

The interior presents a scene of exotic comfort. Not a square inch of wall or ceiling is spared the attentions of Gaudí's imagination – the drawing-room and the dining-room ceiling with its cherry branches of painted stucco are just one example.

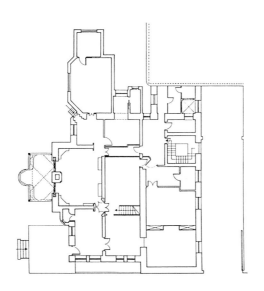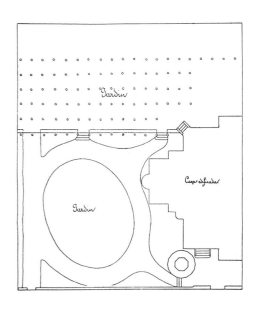

PALAU GÜELL

Antoni Gaudí i Cornet, 1885–1890
Carrer Nou de la Rambla 3 and 5

A site measuring less than 400 square metres is not really adequate for a palace, nor can the surrounding area be described as palatial. But these external criteria shrink to insignificance in the face of a genius like Antoni Gaudí and a generous client like Eusebi Güell i Bacigalupi. The latter was Gaudí's most important patron and later became a close friend. From a humble background, he made his fortune in business in America und then became a member of the Spanish aristocracy, receiving the title of Count. This Catalan patriot, who never forgot his social origins, was not a miser but rather a stylish cosmopolitan figure. The commission represented Gaudí's first major success.

Güell wanted a palatial town house, centrally situated just around the corner from the Ramblas, not far from the docks and not necessarily in the most elegant district. The plot of land in the cramped former Conde del Asalto, measuring no more than 18 metres by 22, had been acquired by Güell specifically for the creation of Barcelona's new top address. It was a difficult commission, but what Gaudí created here would become the ideal venue for receptions, readings and concerts.

Gaudí drew more than 20 alternatives for the design of the main façade. Like Güell, he preferred a clear, symmetrical solution in the Venetian style. An irritatingly novel feature, however, was the inclusion of two parabolic arches at the entrance. The exceedingly fine decorative ironwork between the arches (the Catalan coat of arms) and in the gateways (Güell's monogram), an example of early Art Nouveau, also distracts from the otherwise austerely structured façade.

PALAU GüELL
Rear façade and roofscape

The symmetry of the façade gives little clue to the complication that lies within. The Palau Güell is a paradise of ideas for the exploitation of space. Examples are the vaults in the basement – originally intended for horses and carriages – the drive-in entrance hall which opens up behind the two large gates, but above all, the salon on the first floor. The floor area of this reception room is relatively small, but this is not immediately obvious because of the room's extraordinary height of over 17 metres. It derives its height from a conical tower on the roof terrace which seems to brood over the salon's domed roof. At the same time, small fanlights illuminate the interior, suggesting a starry firmament in broad daylight.

The tower is not the only bizarre shape on the roof. It has company in the form of eighteen curious chimney stacks and ventilation shafts. They were Gaudí's prototypes for his subsequently so famous roof-sculptures on the Casa Batlló and the Casa Milà.

The only ornamentation on the austere rear façade is a projection shrouded in Venetian blinds. Were it not for the surreal roofscape, the building could be taken for a traditional house.

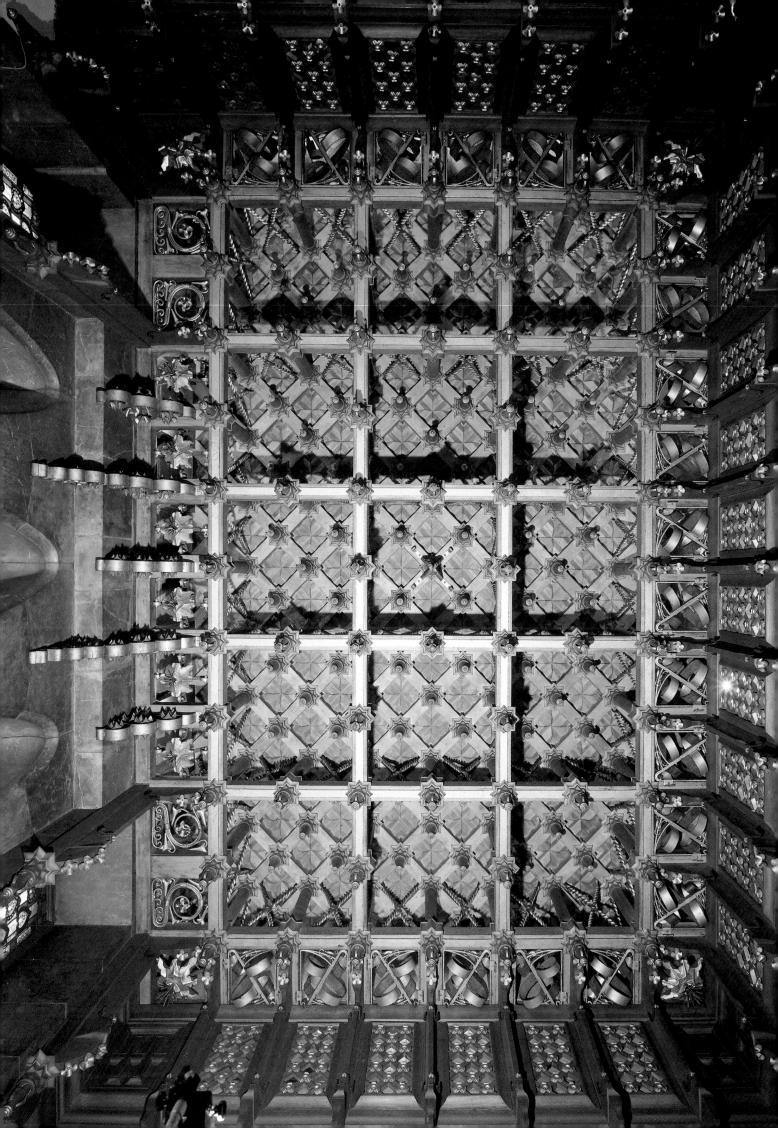

PALAU GÜELL

Living area on the first floor with the
original furnishings; living area ceiling

PALAU GÜELL

Dome over the salon on the first floor; sofa
in the client's bedroom on the second floor

THE HEYDAY OF MODERNISMO

SAGRADA FAMILIA

Francisco de Paula del Villar i Lozano,
1882–1883; Antoni Gaudí i Cornet,
1884–1926
Plaça de la Sagrada Familia

Originally, this church, as designed by Villar, was dominated by neo-Gothic stylistic and compositional elements. However, the commission was soon transferred to Gaudí, who gradually changed the design, until, in a unique process of creation, he had transformed it into one of the most unusual structures of the 20th century. A major part of his life was taken up by this work. He constantly revised his plans, finding new solutions to the problems of detail.

When Gaudí died in 1926, the only part of the building to have been consecrated was the East Front, dedicated to the Nativity of Christ. The work was then continued by his pupils. However, as time passed, the voices of the critics grew louder, because Gaudí's personal signature was fading more and more into the background, and it was, after all, this that had given the church its unique character, achieved after years of personal wrestling with the project. This debate has continued to the present day, and intensified in particular after the appointment in 1986 of Josep Maria Subirach to create modern sculptures for the façades.

SAGRADA FAMILIA PARISH SCHOOL

Antoni Gaudí i Cornet, 1906
Carrer de Mallorca 403

This small school, with its undulating roof, was actually designed as a temporary structure. It represented a quite novel interpretation of the shallow, wide-span Catalan brick vault, and thus became a demonstration piece in itself. In particular, the soft, apparently irregular roof is constructed exclusively of straight elements. Le Corbusier was one of the admirers of this little building, whose simplicity brings together all the originality, organic harmony and dynamism of Gaudí's architecture.

By 1900, Modernismo had asserted itself on a broad scale. As an elitist movement, it aimed particularly at the bourgeoisie. Its rise was concurrent with the development of related artistic styles in Europe: Art Nouveau, Jugendstil, Liberty, Secession, to name the most important. Modernismo was not a unitary movement, free of all adulteration. Simply by virtue of its being a child of its time, it came up with certain marked features which continually recurred, but basically it was a mixture and a development of very different currents and individual contributions.[16] The most far-reaching developments undertaken by Modernismo were in the spheres of architecture and the decorative arts.

Catalan Modernismo had its sights fixed on Paris, the point of orientation for many artists, as well as on the English theoreticians John Ruskin and William Morris, whose writings were available in translation from 1901 onwards. Catalonia at that time was a microcosm, a harmonic whole, and her bourgeoisie exhibited close solidarity. These three factors allowed Modernismo to establish itself as a comprehensive social programme. A kind of common national feeling, extending both to religion and to economic affairs, encouraged an untrammelled exchange of ideas between politicians, artists and industrialists.

There are a number of noteworthy features of Modernismo architecture, whose evolution was confined almost exclusively to Catalonia, and to Barcelona above all. These features manifested themselves in buildings whose composition followed the rules of the Beaux Arts, but sought their own points of reference in the Middle Ages and other historical periods. A very popular motif was the elaborate treatment of masonry – a treatment which underlined the natural beauty of the medium while setting subtle accents of its own.

The most important exponent of Modernismo in architecture was, beyond all doubt, Antoni Gaudí. The Temple de la Sagrada Familia became the hallmark of his extraordinary work. The slow progress of the construction work – Gaudí devoted more than 40 years between 1884 and 1926 to his major project, the only interruption being caused by the First World War[17] – meant that the church evolved parallel to his more mature works and in effect drew together the threads of his final phase of activity.[18] Its most surprising element, the spires with their echoes of clay structures, has nothing to do with Art Nouveau, but rather with natural models and with the indigenous architecture of North Africa. Directly alongside the Sagrada Familia stands the building which Le Corbusier admired most: the little school with the undulating roof (1906).[19]

With the Sagrada Familia still unfinished, Gaudí died, leaving behind a legacy of vehement dispute. Plans were as good as non-existent, because Gaudí's practice was one of constant experimentation. The total project has certainly been

CASA BATLLO

Antoni Gaudí i Cornet, 1904–1907
Passeig de Gràcia 43

Anyone whose time is limited to a crash-course in Modernismo architecture is best advised to go straight to the Passeig de Gràcia. The so-called Disharmonious Block comprises, peacefully united, the Casa Lleó Morera by Domènech i Montaner, the Casa Amatller by Puig i Cadafalch, along with the Casa Batlló and, a little further down, the Casa Milà, both by Gaudí. Direct comparison of the façades brings clearly to light the individual outlooks of these architects, the three most important exponents of Barcelona Modernismo: playful art nouveau in the Casa Lleó Morera, neo-Gothic stepped gable and geometric ornamentation in the Casa Amatller, and organic naturalistic forms in the two buildings designed by Gaudí. When remodelling the Casa Batlló, Gaudí was left a free hand; the client, Josep Batlló i Casanovas, a wealthy textile manufacturer, laid down no prior specifications. The street front was given a totally novel face, a "living" face, so to speak. The "piano nobile", the first floor, rests on an arcade of five arches; the window frames look as if they are modelled in clay, while on the upper floors, the bizarre balconies project like masks from the windows. The mosaic on the gently undulating façade is reminiscent of the skin of some outsize reptile, as is the roof, clad in green ceramic "scales". This roof, incidentally, forms a very cunning bridge between the different heights of the neighbouring buildings.

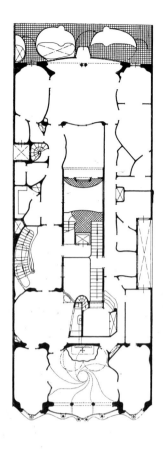

continued as the architect intended, but its contemporary quality has been lost. In his lifetime, Gaudí saw no more than a few fragments completed. What has been built since his death is basically no more than coarse imitation. All of this has inevitably led to a barrage of criticism. Since the mid-1960s the argument has often been made, that over the years the work has degenerated to such an extent that the Sagrada Familia has become a "Cathedral of Kitsch".

The mature phase in Gaudí's œuvre, transcending personal stylistic quirks, was determined by a search for new, lightweight structures that allowed for the creation of large spaces. This was the reason for Gaudí's interest in the structural logic of Gothic architecture. Taking his cue from here, he experimented quite freely and arrived at abstractions of great formal austerity; the whole process, nonetheless, was informed by the natural world, its shapes and structures. In their spatial organization and organic structuring, the roof-terrace of the Casa Milà, the Hall of Columns in the Parc Güell and the unfinished crypt of the Colonia Güell (1898–1915), can be counted amongst his most complex buildings.

Antoni Gaudí's most sensational urban building is the Casa Milà in the Passeig de Gràcia. Built between 1906 and 1910, it is popularly known as the "Pedrera" or "Quarry". It is a highly expressive, generously proportioned complex within the architectural co-ordinates laid down by the Eixample plan. The most significant innovation consists in the abolition of the staircases normally found in apartment blocks. In the Casa Milà the only access – apart from the service stairs – to one's own apartment is the lift. This results in an entirely new kind of inner courtyard. Instead of the usual poky and unhygienic yards, here we have two generously proportioned and extraordinarily organic open spaces. One of the primary concepts underlying Gaudí's ground plans was the free development of lines and forms. This allowed for the arrangement of a diverse sequence of living areas whose convex corridors lead to the inner courtyards, as well as polygonal walls and low, curved ceilings. There are no straight lines in the "Pedrera". The undulating stone façade and the amorphous balcony balustrades, reminiscent of seaweed, conjure up the image of cliffs on which time and the sea have left their mark. The climax of this creative design is reached on the roof-terrace, with its sculptural ventilation shafts and chimneys, whose dynamic, helical forms wander off into the realms of sheer fantasy.

The Parc Güell (1900–1914), commissioned by Gaudí's most important patron, Eusebio Güell, is, of all his projects, the one most strongly anchored in the landscape. This immense ensemble is an authentic universe of the forms and iconologies relating to Gaudí's own personal world: the world of nature, of Christendom, of Catalonia, of the Mediterranean. The work is an effervescent

CASA BATLLO
Façade after its complete
remodelling by Antoni Gaudí; plan

CASA BATLLO
Stairway to the piano nobile

Flowing forms are also dominant in the interior: walls, ceilings, doors, built-in furniture, banisters. Glass doors, skylights and windows glazed with coloured glass provide for a pleasantly subdued light. An unconventional feature is the main staircase in the interior courtyard of the deep, narrow site: in order to admit as much light to the lower storeys as to the upper, the windows are graded in size, becoming smaller as one ascends. Gradated colour tones in the wall-tiles – from light to dark blue – also regulate the intensity of the reflected light.

synthesis, in which newly interpreted classical elements make their appearance,
for example, the Doric colonnade. At the same time, the logic of industrial
mass-production is apparent, as in the meandering benches clad in ceramic
fragments, above the Hall of Columns. In harmony with the biomorphous plas-
ticity which characterizes the architecture of Victor Horta and Hector Guimard,
Gaudí designed a naturalistic, neo-romantic park with a touch both of Wagner
and of Gulliver's Travels.

Gaudí's mature phase also saw the appearance on the Passeig de Gràcia of the
Casa Batlló (1904–1907); in fact the building was already there, but Gaudí
comprehensively redesigned it.[20] The bone-like stone columns, iron balustrades

in the form of masks and the reptilian façade are all due to Gaudí and the striking ridge of the roof is a masterpiece in the way it is integrated into the existing ensemble.

The architects of Modernismo used the homogeneous structure of Cerdà's enlargement and the eclectic architecture of 19th-century builders as the foundation for their own individual and imaginative contributions. But basically their work reveals a rejection of Cerdà's isotropic outline; they would have preferred a city of boulevards, of diagonals, of winding paths and public squares full of irregularities and individual details.

Gaudí's architectural legacy lived on in a series of talented pupils, who, starting out from his naturalistic Modernismo, later developed their own Noucentismo and proto-rationalist styles.[21] In this context we think of Francesc Berenguer, Joan Rubió i Bellvé[22] and in particular of Josep Maria Jujol, though none of his highly individual works – with the exception of the Casa Planells (1923–1924) in the Avinguda Diagonal, and the fountain on the Plaça d'Espanya, built for the 1929 International Exhibition – is actually in Barcelona.[23]

The work of Josep Puig i Cadafalch also reflects an intensive process of evolution. His later historical and archaeological studies, in particular, are of outstanding importance. The Casa Amatller (1898–1900) and the Casa de les Punxes (1903–1905) are two of his most striking buildings dating from the Modernismo period, showing that for him, the process of urbanization began on the scale of the individual house. His work, oriented as it was towards the house and the city, gradually led him to a position where the markedly singular, artistic Modernismo style was left behind in favour of Noucentismo.

The Casaramona industrial complex (1909–1911) is Puig i Cadafalch's most successful and most spectacular work. The extensive factory buildings take up an entire block of Cerdà's plan. The internal spaces are structured by huge vaults of Catalan masonry reinforced by iron tension rods. Two water-towers, whose vertical lines have something of the Gothic about them, set off in contrapuntal manner the horizontal lines of the whole ensemble. Puig i Cadafalch's many and varied activities as an architect, a patron of Catalan culture, a politician and a historian were all parts of a single, coherent plan. It was a wide-ranging project whose success depended on its being approached from different sides. In order to confer legitimacy on autonomous Catalan art and architecture, the political and cultural institutions had to be guided and the spread of historical and archaeological knowledge encouraged. To prove the formal validity of these principles, it was necessary to create exemplary architecture and to influence the structures of the city, the framework of bourgeois life.[24]

CASA AMATLLER

Josep Puig i Cadafalch, 1898–1900
Passeig de Gràcia 41

Like the Casa Batlló, the present Casa Amatller is also the result of altering an existing structure. Puig i Cadafalch – who was not only an architect but also a politician, historian and archaeologist, is regarded as the outstanding exponent of neo-Gothic Modernismo. The undulating forms and opulent ornamentation of the more familiar Art Nouveau give way in his work to geometric patterns, while the colours and materials associated with Modernismo – such as sgraffiti – are retained. The façade of the Casa Amatller also has allusions to Catalan Gothic, for example, in the balconies and windows on the second and fourth floors and in the arcades on the ground and third floors, which Cadafalch combined with elegant stylistic elements of the Dutch architectural tradition, cladding the stepped gable with coloured ceramic tiles. Also worthy of special note are the sculptures by Eusebi Arnau in the entrance porch and above the balconies.

Today the building is the headquarters of the Institute of Spanish Art, and the hallway is open to visitors wishing to inspect the glass mosaics and the splendid chandeliers, the ceramics and the sculptures.

CASA AMATLLER

Details of the stairwell;
lamp on the piano nobile

Sala d'Actes
◀

CASA MACAYA

Josep Puig i Cadafalch, 1899–1901;
Jaume Bach, Gabriel Mora, 1989
Passeig de Sant Joan 106

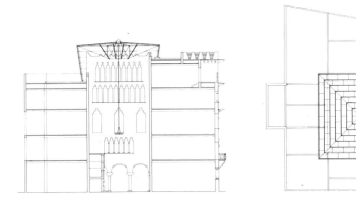

CASA MACAYA

Details of the street façade and the inner courtyard

While rebuilding this house, Puig i Cadafalch followed the design principles applied at the Casa Amatller. Both projects are regarded as prime examples of his Modernismo phase.

Both the large inner courtyard with its staircase, the white stucco façade and the wrought-iron railings are reminiscent of Renaissance buildings in Valencia or Palma de Mallorca. In particular, the sgraffiti of the Casa Macaya are early harbingers of the tendency towards a notion of design based on local traditions, a notion which in its populist Noucentismo version was later to have a decisive influence on his work.

After further rebuilding by Jaume Bach and Gabriel Mora, the Casa Macaya now houses the cultural centre of the Caixa de Pensions, one of Spain's leading banks. Their most spectacular alteration was the installation of an inverted glass and steel pyramid over the inner courtyard.

CASA TERRADES

Josep Puig i Cadafalch, 1903–1905
Avinguda Diagonal 416–420

The site occupied by the Casa Terrades is in the form of an irregular hexagon. Puig i Cadafalch designed a self-contained complex whose corners are marked by round towers of various heights, each topped by sharply pointed conical spires, to which the building owes its nickname of Casa de les Punxes, or House of Spires. The towers and façades point to the Gothic town houses of central Europe as a source of inspiration, but Puig also introduced elements of the Catalan architectural tradition. It is the combination and reinterpretation of these elements which enable us to classify this as a Modernismo design.

111

CASARAMONA FACTORY

Josep Puig i Cadafalch, 1909–1911
Carrer de Mèxic 36–44

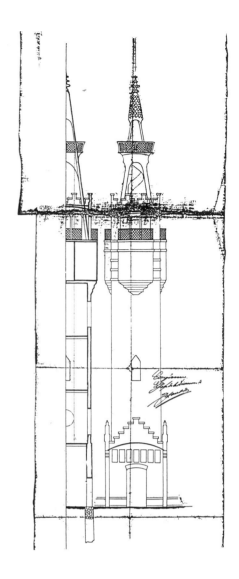

This project, a late work by Puig i Cadafalch, consists of a huge industrial complex complete with inner courtyards and
streets. When it was built, the surrounding
area was in open country, but the grounds
now border on the 1929 World Exhibition
site. The buildings cover the area of one of
Cerdà's blocks. Halls with shallow brick
vaults on a grid of metal supports form a
square, truncated at the corners. The "pin-
nacles" along the façades and the two tall
water-towers lend the complex some of
the character of a mediaeval fortress.
After the Civil War, production came to a
halt, and thereafter the complex served as
a police barracks. Recently it has been acquired by a bank, whose intention is to
use it as a major arts centre.

GASWORKS

Josep Domènech i Estapà, 1906
Passatge del Gasòmetre

The Passatge del Gasòmetre was one of
those "backyards" of Barcelona along the
coast which were once dominated by industrial buildings and warehouses, but
which are currently undergoing drastic
transformation as a result of implementa-
tion of the development plans for Barceloneta and the Poble Nou. The water-
tower of the former gasworks, along with
the ironwork of the gasometer, will, however, be preserved.

114

VALLVIDRERA MOUNTAIN RAILWAY
STATION

Bonaventura Conill, Arau Calvet, 1905
Carrer de Queralt 20

The clearly structured, sparingly decorated
white cube on a pedestal of natural stone-
work is reminiscent of the suburban stations on the Vienna City Railway, designed by Otto Wagner. On the street side,
the main and side entrances, and the
ground floor window, all display the parabolic arch so popular with Art Nouveau
architects.

HOSPITAL DE LA SANTA CREU I DE SANT PAU

Lluís Domènech i Montaner, 1902–1911;
Pere Domènech i Roura, 1913–1923
Avinguda de Sant Antoni Maria Claret 167–171

The Hospital de la Santa Creu i de Sant Pau was the result of a bequest to the city of Barcelona by the banker Pau Gil i Serra, whose will provided for a legacy of four million pesetas for a hospital which was to be named after him. The foundation stone was laid on 15th February 1902, and to start with, building went ahead briskly. But by 1911, the bequest had been used up, only eight of a planned total of 48 buildings having been con-structed, and even these were not usable, as they still lacked roofs. Negotiations then started between the executors of the will and the hospital management, to whom, on condition the complex was completed as planned, all rights were transferred. Additional land was pur-chased and the work proceeded with vi-gour. Thanks not least to private dona-tions, and with the proceeds from the sale of the old hospital, the central building and the chapel were completed. Two con-struction phases can be clearly discerned. In the first, between 1902 and 1911 under Lluís Domènech, Modernismo tendencies still dominate, for example in the brick cu-polas, the vegetal ornamentation and the ceramics.

HOSPITAL DE LA SANTA CREU
Vaulted ceiling in the entrance

Following the death of Lluís Domènech i
Montaner, direction of the project was
taken over by his son, who eventually decided on a middle path between loyalty to
the original plans drawn up by his father
and the new trends which sought to put
Art Nouveau behind them. Thus it is that
the convent, the pharmacy, the kitchens
and above all the convalescent home
show his own eclectic taste and his incli-
nation towards the Baroque.

Among the numerous individual buildings
which constitute the total complex, the
wards in the pavilions are of particular
note. The pavilions all differ a little from
each other, although their basic structures
are the same, and they are connected by a
clever system of tunnels. The layout of
these pavilions permits direct access to the
gardens, as well as ensuring good ventilation and optimum exploitation of available
sunlight.

As long ago as 1930, but especially in
1961, at a time when Modernismo was
not greatly admired, comprehensive, and
unfortunately somewhat infelicitous rebuilding was carried out, which destroyed
a great deal, in particular of the interiors.
Only in the most recent restoration, dating
from 1979 and 1980, was a more sensitive
approach to this highly individual ensemble adopted, and an attempt made to
combine the demands of a modern hospital with the preservation of an architectural work of great originality.

123

CASA LLEO MORERA

Lluís Domènech i Montaner, 1902–1906
Passeig de la Gràcia 35

Like the Casa Amatller and the Casa Batlló, its fellows in the trio which constitute the "Unharmonious Block", the Casa Lleó Morera on the corner of the Passeig de la Gràcia and the Carrer del Consell de Cent is the result of the conversion of an existing building. When Lluís Domènech designed the new façades and interiors, he was at the peak of his Modernismo phase. His imagination in the creation of new floral ornamentation, whether painted – as on the foyer ceiling – or in stone, stucco, wood, glass or ceramics, seemed to know no bounds. Domènech's architecture at the time was also receiving a measure of official recognition, and for the Casa Lleó Morera, as later for the Palau de la Música Catalana and the Hospital de la Santa Creu i de Sant Pau, he was honoured with awards from the city of Barcelona.

Alongside the opulent, delicately-worked decor – which nonetheless keeps to well-ordered patterns – what strikes the beholder is the unconventional articulation of the façades. Balconies and oriels in the form of circular segments of different sizes alternate with long sections of balustrade. Window niches and balconies are decorated with sculptures by Eusebi Arnau. On the roof, the corner of the house is given additional emphasis by a ceramic-covered stone crown.

Until 1943, the Casa Lleó Morera was in the possession of the family. Following its sale to an insurance company, the ground floor was converted into shops, and thereby totally destroyed. Only in recent years have there been efforts to restore the building on the basis of the original plans.

CASA LLEO MORERA

Details of piano nobile rooms

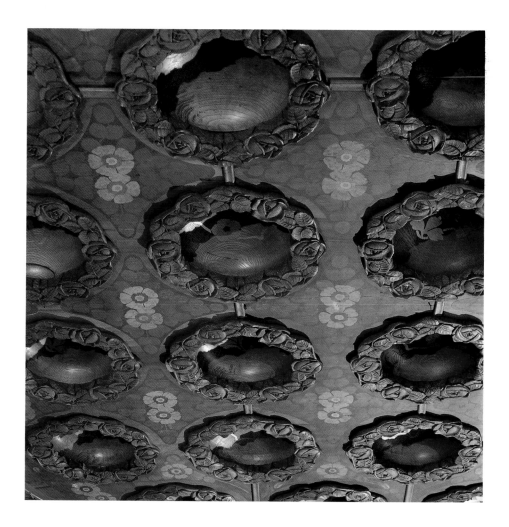

All the interior decoration was carried out by Gaspar Homar together with the sculptors Eusebi Arnau and Joan Carreras, and the painter Josep Pey. The mosaics are the work of Mario Maragliano and Lluís Bru Salelles, the glass work is by Joan Rigalt and Jeroni Granell and the ceramics by Antoni Serra Fiter.

CASA LLEO MORERA

Glass wall to the inner courtyard by Josep Pey; the chairs at the table are of the "Gaulino" pattern designed in 1987 by Oscar Tusquets

Today the decorative setting of the Casa Lleó Morera is the home of the City Tourist Office. Even for those not in need of specific information, however, a visit is worthwhile, if only because of the apparently endless variety of the Art Nouveau decoration.

CASA QUERALTO (left)

Josep Plantada i Artigas, 1906–1907
Rambla de Catalunya 88

CASA FUSTER

Lluís Domènech i Montaner 1908–1910
Passeig de Gràcia 132

The Casa Fuster was Domènech's last
work and represents a synthesis of his creative expression. As in the previous buildings, he incorporated both regional and international stylistic elements here.

131

PALAU DE LA MUSICA CATALANA

Lluís Domènech i Montaner, 1905–1908;
Tusquets, Díaz & Associates, 1982–1989
Carrer de Sant Pere més alt 11

PALAU DE LA MUSICA CATALANA

Views of the extension; mosaic

In 1904 a plan was formed to provide the "Orfeó Català" choral society, founded by Lluís Millet and Amadeu Vives, with an auditorium of its own. The chosen site, a small, irregularly shaped plot of land, lies hidden away between two streets in the old city, not far from the Via Laietana. Magnificent and luxuriant in its decoration, the street façades of the Palau present themselves to public view on both sides of the massive corner section with its sculptured allegory of the "Catalan People's Song", the work of Miquel Blay, the outstanding Modernismo sculptor. Busts of Bach, Beethoven, Wagner and Palestrina rest on the tops of pillars projecting from the façades. Further down, on the level of the first-floor balustrades, the pillars are covered in coloured mosaics. The foyer, auditorium and stage are arranged as a sequence. The auditorium is illuminated by a coloured-glass dome in the centre, composed of numerous facets and consisting of concave sections. The motifs of the façade decoration are recapitulated inside, in a yet more lavish style. Floral and vegetal patterns in ever new variants cover the ceilings and walls, complemented by columns heavy with symbolism.

The 1980s saw a highly successful restoration, rebuilding and enlargement of the Palau de la Música by Oscar Tusquets and Carlos Díaz. The underlying plan provided for a reduction in the size of the nave of the adjacent Church of Sant Francesc de Paula, which had been designed by E. P. Cendoya in 1940, but never completed for lack of money. The resulting extra space was converted into a little square with a new access to the Palau. The rear façade had a glass wall put up in front of it, and the foyer was thus enlarged. Office and other ancillary rooms, hitherto housed here, were transferred to the newly-built annex with its striking round tower.

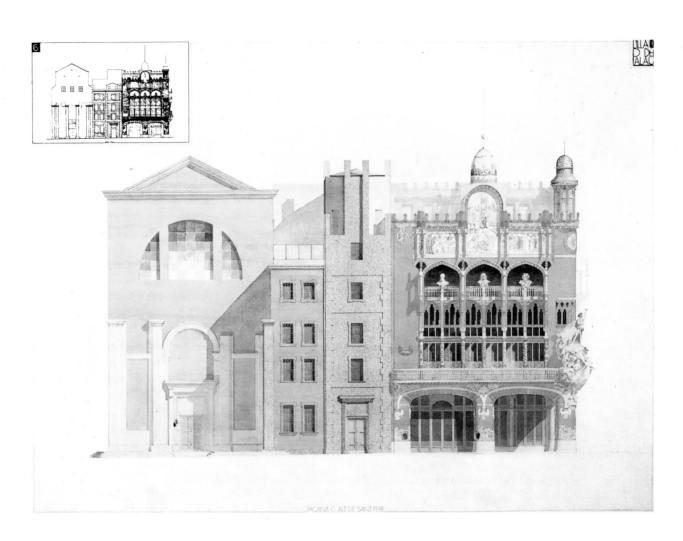

FAÇANA C. ALT DE SANT PERE

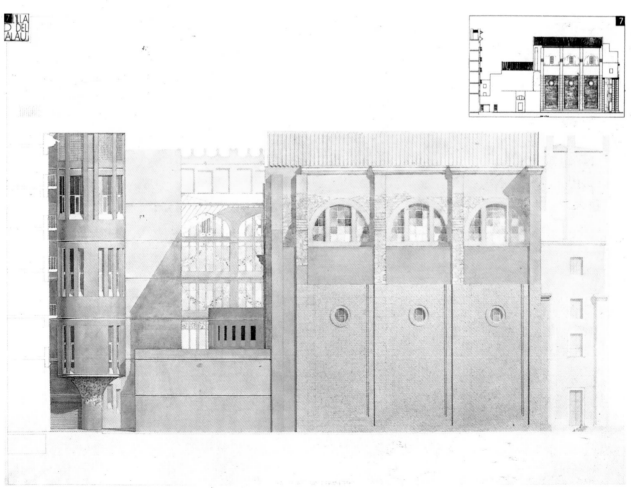

Columns on the façade facing the Carrer de
Sant Pere més alt; round tower of the annex
on the Carrer Sant Francesc de Paula

The two upper storeys of the round tower
of the annex now house the Palau de la
Música's library. Above it is installed the
building's air-conditioning system. The
glass and steel structure is a skilful visual
bridge to Lluís Domènech's floral ornamentation.

PALAU DE LA MUSICA CATALANA

Foyer by Lluís Domènech i Montaner;
new approach to the Palau, and
extension of the foyer, by Tusquets,
Díaz & Associates.

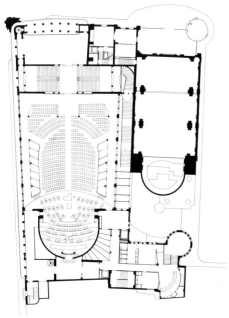

CASA DAMIANS

Eduard Ferrés i Puig, Lluís Homs i Moncusi,
Agusti Mas, 1913–1915
Carrer de Pelai 54

CASA TOSQUELLA

Eduard Maria Balcells i Buigas, 1906
Carrer de Vallirana 93

LA ROTONDA

Adolf Ruiz i Casamitjana, 1906
Passeig de Sant Gervasi 51

CASA CABOT

Josep Vilaseca i Casanovas, 1901–1904
Roger de Llúria 8–14

Four Art Nouveau buildings, yet each very different: depicted here are the parapet on the façade of the Casa Cabot, an otherwise inconspicuous block of flats; the playful structure on the roof of the "Rotonda", a former grand hotel; the Casa Tosquella, with its Moorish inspiration, now an enchanting, overgrown ruin; and the Casa Damians, reminiscent of Secession buildings.

CASA MILA

Antoni Gaudí i Cornet, 1905–1910
Passeig de Gràcia 92

"La Pedrera" – the "Quarry" – as the Casa Milà is sometimes known, is surely the most extravagant extreme that still manages to fit into the homogeneous grid of the Eixample. Gaudí exploited the corner situation to design a façade unique in the history of architecture and one which has had no successors remotely comparable. In clear allusion to the rules of composition applied by the architects of the Baroque, the various elements merge seamlessly into each other, forming a unique unity from amorphous and dynamic shapes. Walls, columns, balconies and windows, together make up a totality in stone, and are set off only by Josep Maria Jujol's wrought-iron balcony balustrades. The Milà family, the owners of the building, at first concurred with Gaudí's idea of placing an enormous image of the Madonna on the corner; this would have been in accordance both with his taste and with his convictions. However, when the building was finished, this plan was abandoned – much to the distress of the architect – for fear of the anti-clerical tendencies which were beginning to organize in the late 19th century.

CASA MILA

Inner courtyard; plan

It was not just in the façades that Gaudí
displayed his innovative powers; the
ground-plan of the building was no less
original. The typical square-shaped inner
courtyards were replaced by two generously proportioned irregularly shaped
courts. Furthermore, the interior of every
apartment forms an organically harmonious continuum, the whole structure
being supported on columns. The building
is crowned by an accessible roofscape of
chimney-stacks and ventilation shafts in
the form of anthropomorphic sculptures.

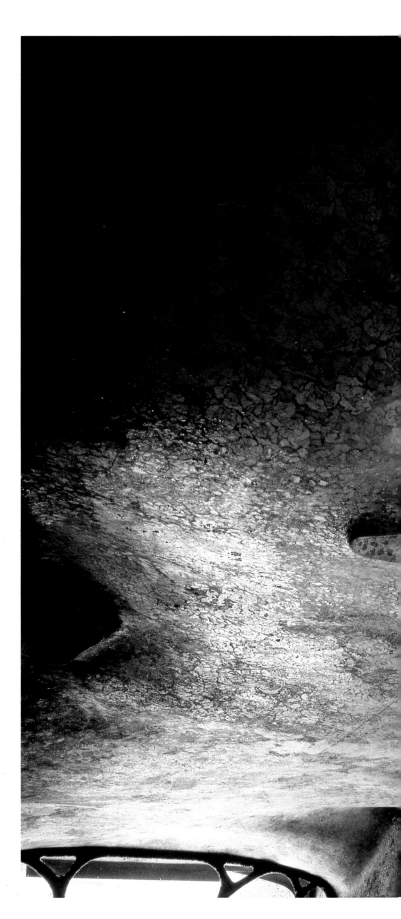

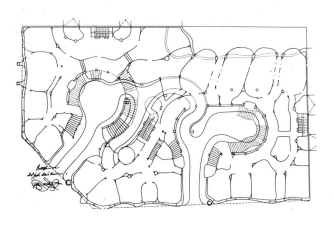

CASA MILA

Drawing-room of the Milà family around 1917, and an apartment in the Casa Milà today

Visibly unimpressed by the futuristic character of the building, the Milà family furnished their own apartment according to the ideas of bourgeois comfort prevailing in the late 19th century: heavy carpets, the individual pieces of furniture self-consciously "arranged", the obligatory palm, decorative art on little tables, columns, and, with the cast of the Nike of Samothrace, also a touch of classical solemnity. The present-day furnishings of one apartment in the Casa Milà seem to suffer from no such horror vacui: an ambience reduced to a minimum of furniture and objets d'art: a dining table, of the "Pedrera" pattern, with chairs designed by Carlos Riart and christened "Fernando" after the apartment's occupant; a delicate side-table by Lluís Clotet; a lamp by Philippe Starck, which does justice to its name, "And suddenly the earth shook", by falling over in response to vibrations.

CASA MILA

Attic conversion by Francesc Joan Barba
i Corsini, 1955

In the mid 1950s the attic storage space
in the Casa Milà was converted into four-
teen apartments whose originality stems
primarily from the high vaults. Antoni
Gaudí's roof design, with its rhythmically
ordered, fan-shaped masonry arches became a feature of Corsini's design, given
additional emphasis by a coat of gleaming
white plaster. The units are all different,
and some have been made into maison-
ettes. There is barely a right angle to be
found in any of the rooms. The exterior
walls have in some cases been left in their
unplastered state, while the newly erected
interior walls are mostly in unplastered
brickwork.

PARC GÜELL

Antoni Gaudí i Cornet, 1900–1914
Carrer d'Olot

The site of what is now the Parc Güell, without a doubt Gaudí's most innovative work, was originally designated for a large-scale housing development. Sixty plots had been marked out on the hillside, offering an outstanding view of the city below. However the scheme, initiated by Eusebi Güell i Bacigalupi, came to nothing, and only the park would be laid out on this hilly, barren site. In 1922 the park fell under the jurisdiction of the city council. The paths through the park either follow the contours of the terrain or are dug out of the slopes in a manner reminiscent of caves. The earth "roofs" are supported by walls and pillars of coarse stone – their angle depending, as in other works by Gaudí, on the direction of the static forces. The centrepiece and "forum" of the proposed housing estate was a broad, level terrace, and it was indeed built. Its balustrade, undulating like an enormous snake, includes a stone bench along the whole of its length. The whole structure, bench and parapet alike, is covered in a mosaic of ceramic fragments and pieces of glass, which serves quite literally as "decus et tutamen". The design of the mosaic was chiefly the work of Josep Maria Jujol. This terrace is supported on Doric columns, which themselves form a kind of hall of columns rearing out of the earth. At the lower staircase, the main entrance is dominated by a ceramic dragon.

The whole park is animated by its unrestrained and inexhaustible formal, symbolic and plastic energy and by its inimitable synthesis of architecture and natural setting. In 1984 the Parc Güell, along with the Casa Milà and the Palau Güell, was designated by UNESCO as a cultural heritage site worthy of special protection.

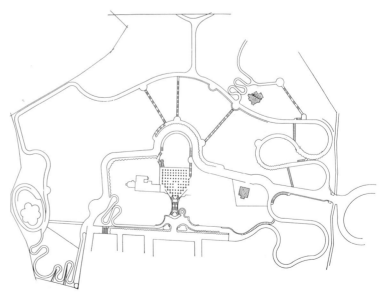

Details of the benches; detail of the Hall
of Columns

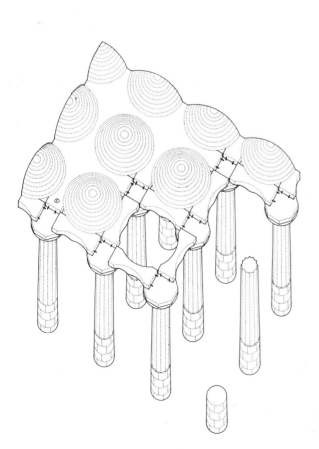

CASA COMALAT

Salvador Valeri i Pupurull, 1906–1911
Avinguda Diagonal 442

A building with two very different faces: the main façade is characterized by playful Rococo motifs, while the rear façade overlooking the Carrer de Còrsega is covered in bulging projections and ceramic ornamentation.

In 1889 the Barcelona Ajuntament decided to adopt a city plan drawn up ten years earlier by Angel Josep Baixeras, which among other things provided for a rapid road link between the Eixample and the docks.

Referred to as Grand Via A in Baixeras' plan, it was opened in 1907 under the name of Via Laietana. A high price had to be paid, however, for this road link: parts of the old city were destroyed to make room for prestigious administrative buildings.

CAIXA DE PENSIONS

Enric Sagnier i Villavecchia, 1917–1918
Via Laietana 56–58, Carrer de les Jonqueres 2

Enric Sagnier was also responsible for the
Duana Nova, the new Customs House on
the Passeig de Colom completed in 1895,
and for the massive complex of the Palau
de Justícia on the Passeig de Lluís Companys, which was built between 1887 and
1908. Here, on the Carrer de les Jonqueres, where it joins the Via Laietana,
and on the Via Laietana itself, he built two
office blocks for the Caixa de Pensions.
They are late works in the Modernismo
style, which by this time was well past its
heyday.

PLAÇA DE TOROS "MONUMENTAL"

Ignasi Mas i Morell, 1913–1915
Gran Via de les Corts Catalanes 749

PLAÇA DE TOROS DE "LES ARENES"

August Font i Carreras, 1899–1900
Gran Via de les Corts Catalanes 387

The designs of both these bullrings, as was
fashionable in late 19th-century Barcelona
architecture, borrow elements of Islamic
building styles. The "Monumental" today
houses the Museu Taurí.

FARMACIA PALOMAS

Fèlix Cardellach, 1907
Ronda de Sant Pere 40

PLA DE LA BOQUERIA

La Rambla

FARMACIA PADRELL (left)
Carrer de Sant Pere més baix 52

BAR MUY BUENAS (right)
Carrer del Carme 63

The degree of popularity attained by Modernismo in Barcelona in the early years of the century can best be judged by the numerous shops in this style along the Rambles, in the narrow lanes of the old city, or in the heart of the Eixample. Among the best preserved are pharmacies, with extravagant glazing and mosaics, rich floral carvings and highly imaginative wrought ironwork. However they were not alone: shops providing for everyday needs, such as bakeries, also sought the attention of an affluent clientele by such means as colourful faïence tiles, marble-topped counters and etched mirrors.

CASA FIGUERAS (right)

Antoní Ros i Güell, 1902
La Rambla 83

KIOSK

Rambla de Canaletes

FARMACIA PALOMAS

Fèlix Cardellach, 1907
Ronda de Sant Pere 40

FARMACIA PUIGORIOL

Marià Pau, Francesc Torres, 1914
Carrer de Mallorca 312

FARMACIA ARUMI

La Rambla 121

FARMACIA DEL CARMEN

Riera Alta, Carrer del Carme

FARMACIA VILARDELL

Gran Via de les Corts Catalanes 650

CASA TEIXIDOR

M.J. Raspall, 1909
Ronda de Sant Pere 16

FORN SARRET

Carrer de Girona 73

WOLF'S (right)

Carrer de Ferran 7

IV

NOUCENTISMO AND RATIONALISM

BENEDICTINE MONASTERY

Nicolau Maria Rubió i Tudurí, 1922–1936;
Raimon Duran i Reynals, c. 1940
Carretera d'Esplugues 101

A building, seemingly set in Tuscany,
clearly influenced by the brilliant Floren-
tine architect Filippo Brunelleschi, a mas-
ter of the early Renaissance. In designing
it thus, Nicolau Maria Rubió was fulfilling
the wishes of his clients regarding the new
monastery. This was no easy task, because
he had two clients to deal with: on the
one hand, the Benedictine community of
Montserrat, which wished for something
reminiscent of the origins of the order –
dating from the 6th century; and on the
other, the financial patron Nicolau d'Ol-
zina, who – according to Rubió, in common with most of the Catalan bourgeoisie
at the time – wanted a building in the Renaissance style. "In order to satisfy both
parties, I began with a Graeco-Roman Tus-
can order, and proceeded to Brunelleschi … By making the vaulted structure of
the nave clearly apparent on the façade, I
was following the architectural ideas current at the time of Bramante." Finally, cau-
tious allusions to the language of Michel-
angelo – and thus to the transcending of
the Renaissance – were introduced by
Rubió in the design of the cloisters which
flank the church.

172

ONTIS · SERRATI · DEIPARÆ · SACRVM

"RAMON LLULL" SCHOOL COMPLEX

Josep Goday i Casals 1918–1923
Avinguda Diagonal 269–275

The process of development leading from Modernismo to so-called Noucent-ismo in the early years of the century involved no drastic break with the past. Puig i Cadafalch along with some of his contemporaries came up with architectural solutions which toned down the mediaeval influences and attached importance once more to classical methods and elements. While Modernismo identified itself with a style whose roots lay in the Middle Ages, Noucentismo was based on the assumption that Catalan identity had its origins in the balanced sobriety of Classicism and in the Mediterranean character. While for Gaudí the Mediterranean stood for the organic and the earthy, for the adherents of Noucentismo it was the symbol of moderation, of purity of proportion, and of classic forms. While Modernismo was inspired by the ideal of the artistic rebel and individualist, Noucentismo encouraged a picture of the artist as one working within society, a society indeed which was to be ennobled by art, culture and education. Startling villas and public buildings gradually gave way to parks, libraries and schools. The Mancomunitat de Catalunya, a relatively autonomous association of Catalan provincial authorities, which was active between 1913 and 1925, encouraged these projects as part of a didactic planning policy that was both urbane and down-to-earth.[25]

This architecture, which in Catalonia tended towards Proto-Rationalism, Mediterraneanism and Neo-Brunelleschianism, was in tune with architectural developments in other European countries. One needs only to think of the work of Tony Garnier and Léon Jaussely in France, Heinrich Tessenow in Germany or the Novecentismo movement in Milan.

One of the most important Noucentismo architects in Barcelona was Josep Goday, who was responsible for the school complexes of Ramon Llull (1918–1923) and Collasso i Gil (1932). Another member of the group was Adolf Florensa, with his grand buildings on the Via Laietana.[26]

It was during this period that Puig i Cadafalch planned the Alfonso XIII and Victoria Eugenia Exhibition Buildings for the World Exhibition of 1929. This exhibition, which had been planned as early as 1913 for the electrical industry, was in many ways a demonstration of the variety of paths being trodden by Noucentismo. Noucentismo stood side by side with a monumental style based on the continuing presence of a strong, late academic influence. This is seen most clearly in Pedro Cendoya and Enric Catà's Palau Nacional.

A particularly conspicuous exception at this exhibition was the German State Pavilion, which was designed by Ludwig Mies van der Rohe. This was a manifesto which symbolized not only international progress but also the birth of modern architecture in Catalonia. It had been planned merely as a temporary

POBLE ESPANYOL

Francesc Folguera, Ramon Reventós, Xavier Nogués, Miguel Utrillo, 1926–1929
Parc de Montjuïc, Avinguda del Marquès de Comillas

The idea was simple and attractive. To mark the 1929 World Exhibition, representative examples of Spanish architecture of various epochs and from various regions were to be reconstructed at Montjuïc. To this end, the architects Folguera and Reventós, along with the painter Nogués and the critic Utrillo, travelled the length and breadth of the country in search of suitable models.

Thus there arose in this "Spanish Village", alongside mediaeval buildings of the Asturias, typical Andalusian patios, mudéjar mosques and Castilian nobles' palaces – and of course there had to be a Plaça Major, the most important meeting-place in any town. The austerity with which the planners set about their work prevented the project from descending to the level of folklore.

The village remained standing after the Exhibition had closed, and developed into a popular tourist attraction.
Today's night-owls are attracted by the two entrance towers of the Poble Espanyol – replicas of the Torres de Avila – which were converted in the late 1980s by Alfredo Arribas, Miguel Morte and Javier Mariscal into a fantastical night-life centre.

TRAFFIC LINK PLAN

Léon Jaussely, 1917

With his entry, submitted under the name
of Romulus, Jaussely won the public competition, which ran from 1903 to 1904, for
a plan to link Barcelona with the neighbouring towns. The project was never carried out, but had a decisive influence on
the subsequent planning of the city. The
design was in total contradiction to
Cerdà's plan, but entirely in accord with
Modernismo's striving for rationality and
Noucentismo's yearning for monumentality. In response to Cerdà's abstract and
utopian idea of a homogeneous and isotropic network, Jaussely proposed a city
which would reflect the actual power
structures, contradictions and multiformity
of an early 20th-century capitalist society.
Cerdà's layout merged into another network with radial intersections, diagonal
routes, boulevards, exposed complexes
and a complicated concentric layout of
ring-roads with garden city estates.

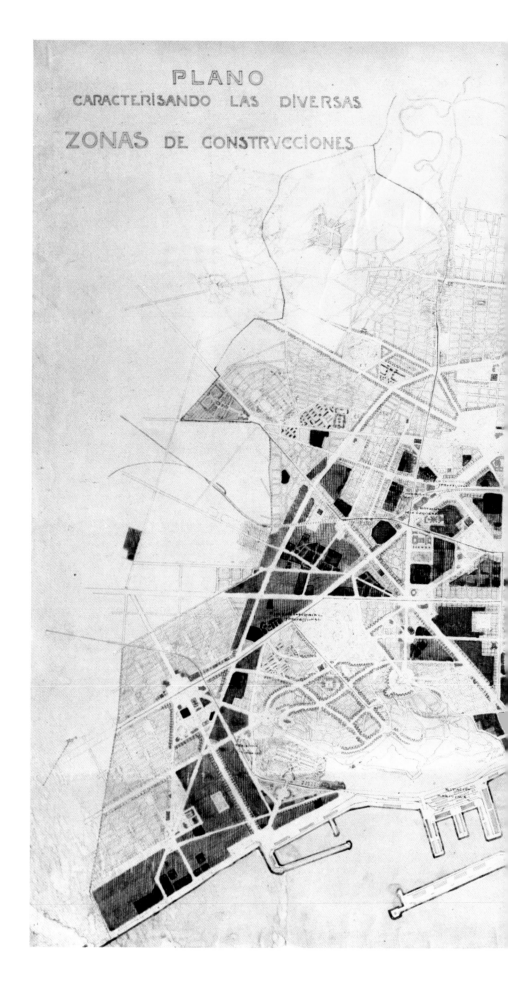

CASAL SANT JORDI

Francesc Folguera i Grassi, 1929–1931
Carrer de Casp 24–26

This building is regarded as an exemplary change in the visual appearance of the area and one which documents the change witnessed by Barcelona at the turn of the century away from historicism and towards rationalist and avant-garde ideals. Folguera had worked out a number of variations for the design of the façade, but decided in the end in favour of a proto-rationalist solution. This building is also one of the very first examples of an attempt to erect a high-rise building in Barcelona. It not only towers over the adjacent houses; its upper storeys also contain a number of south-facing terraces, arcades, pools and galleries hidden from the street. The first three floors above the base contained offices, while the four upper storeys were for residential apartments. The financial backers, the Espona family, had their own apartment in the roof storey. Restoration carried out in 1988 has given new emphasis to one of the most attractive of its features: the large triangular courtyard with glass blocks, which gives more life to the building's interior.

exhibition structure, but this so-called Barcelona Pavilion was dismantled within the space of just a few months. In 1985, an exact replica was erected on precisely the same spot.

The Exhibition area also symbolized the regionalistic currents which characterized Spain in the years between 1910 and 1930. One example is the Poble Espanyol, designed by Miquel Utrillo, Francesc Folguera, Ramon Reventós and Xavier Nogués: a credible and intelligent reconstruction of typical Spanish building styles from Andalusia, Galicia and the Basque country. The architects succeeded in creating an urban environment which, with its streets and squares, was no less lively than it was authentic.[27] These same years saw a mixture of building styles, and one and the same architect would manage to turn himself to late Modernismo, Regionalism, Noucentismo, Art Déco or Proto-Rationalism as the case demanded. Thus Rubió i Bellvé, a pupil of Gaudí's, was able to execute work at the Universidad Industrial which has all the features of Noucentismo. With his Myrurgia factory (1928–1930), Antoni Puig i Gairalt created a building which occupies a stylistic position somewhere between Noucentismo, Art Déco and Rationalism. It was at this time that Francesc Folguera designed the Casal Sant Jordi (1929–1931) for one of the most important street corners of the Eixample. Its unique character, along with its height, made it the first building, in many respects, to which the description "skyscraper" is appropriate.

The purest example of Neo-Brunelleschianism is probably the Benedictine monastery in the Pedralbes district, designed by Raimon Duran i Reynals and Nicolau Maria Rubió i Tudurí, the latter being one of the most versatile of all Catalan architects. He was a pupil of Jean C.N. Forestier, and together with him was responsible for a series of parks, until he later turned to projects of his own, in the process formulating a new theory on the layout of Mediterranean gardens, described in his book *El jardín meridional: Estudio de su trazado y plantación* (*The meridional garden: a study of it's design and planting*, 1934). Through his gardens, Rubió i Tudurí succeeded in giving both the Barcelona townscape and a number of Catalan coastal stretches an inimitable character, unparalleled at the time, and only taken up again under the new, democratic town-planning of the 1980s. He himself suffered the thoroughly undeserved fate of falling into oblivion.[28]

The clear traces left by Noucentismo in Barcelona in the early years of this century are still extant today. For this heritage Barcelona has its relations with a city like Milan to thank, whose own architecture was much influenced by Novecentismo.

The growth of Barcelona also encompassed the rural centres of her immediate hinterland – Gràcia, Sarrià, Les Corts, Sant Andreu and Sant Gervasi, to name but a few. In order to link these new districts more closely with the city, the council invited entries to a competition in 1903, which was eventually won by the French architect Léon Jaussely. As it happened, his plan was not in fact carried out, but it did exercise a considerable influence. This can be seen not least in the city's bypasses, whose orbital layout comes very close to Jaussely's concept.

At the same time, in 1907, the Via Laietana was opened to traffic, having been designed by Angel Baixeras on the basis of the Plan de Reforma de Barcelona. At that time it was the only direct road link between the Eixample and the docks. The tall buildings on either side were influenced by the Noucentismo style, and to a lesser extent, the Chicago school. There was, however, a high price to pay for this traffic artery with its high façade walls: part of the Old Town was demolished, and a demarcation line drawn, behind which a decline set in.

In the late twenties, Catalan architecture drew closer to the uncompromising avant-garde in other parts of Europe: the divide between developments in Barcelona and the latest trends in other great cities such as Paris, Frankfurt or Vienna grew narrower. There arose an ever stronger awareness that traditional Catalan architecture required considerable impulses from the Modernists if it were to overcome the tired academic style and the stage-like townscaping of the turn of the century. Of all the great architects, Le Corbusier was the most admired. He visited Barcelona and collaborated on a plan to modernize the city's layout. This so-called Pla Macià (1933), which was drawn up during the period of the Second Republic in Spain, was dedicated to the then President of the Generalitat, Catalan's regional government. The idea behind this plan was the new theory of "zoning", whereby the city was to be given a new geometric order based on Cerdà's layout and enormous residential blocks.[29]

Young architects such as Josep Lluís Sert, Josep Torres i Clavé, Sixt Illescas, Germàn Rodríguez Arias and others, joined together in an association known as GATCPAC (Grupo de Artistas y Técnicos Catalanes para el Progreso de la Arquitectura Contemporánea), a grouping of Catalan artists and engineers devoted to promoting contemporary architecture. This avant-garde association later inspired the founding of the so-called GATEPAC at the national level, which was in turn was affiliated to CIAM.[30]

This phase was only of short duration, being ended abruptly by the outbreak of the Spanish Civil War (1936–1939). In the few years of its existence a small number of mostly minor building projects was realized, urban fragments, so to

Cabarets enjoyed a boom in the 1930s. Among the most popular was "La Casita Blanca" on the Avinguda del Parallel. A cool atmosphere for hot nights was provided by the "Bar Automatic Continental", a work by the architect Manuel Casas Lamolla dating from 1932.

speak, which could have been effective as models for more general schemes. The most important buildings from this period are the Casa Bloc in Sant Andreu (1932–1936), a complex of linked blocks of Spartan austerity, reminiscent of Le Corbusier; the Dispensari Antituberculós (1934–1938), a tuberculosis clinic in the Old City; and the apartment block on the Carrer de Muntaner (1930–1931). Rodríguez Arias designed two further buildings for the city: the Edificio Astoria (1933–1934) and the building on the Plaça Gala Placídia (1931).[31]

In the words of Eugeni d'Ors, the Barcelona of Modernismo was still a city of the "haute bourgeoisie", while the Noucentismo city had, as a result of immigration on a massive scale, expanded in an unbridled and uncontrolled fashion. D'Ors became a determined advocate of a cultured bourgeois society and promoted the idea of consciously selecting those who might be allowed to take up residence in the city. Behind his unconcealed demand for an elitist culture there hid, when all is said and done, a yearning for a return to a pristine purity and a Mediterranean character which had long since passed into history.

Just for a few years, then, between 1930 and 1936, did Barcelona take on the characteristics and contrasts of a 20th-century European city where the leading architects of the European Modern movement – Le Corbusier, Ludwig Hilberseimer, Ernst May and others – would seek to realize their plans. Within GATC-PAC there were discussions of a "city of the masses" in which the proletariat would play an active role. It came up with ideas about complexes to be built in the vicinity of Barcelona, such as a proposed "Ciudad de reposo y vacaciones", or "rest and recuperation city", to serve the leisure needs of the working classes. The social, economic and town planning ideas which were being aired during the period of the Spanish Republic had much in common with the progressive notions fashionable during the inter-war period. However, while in the rest of Europe the supporters of these ideas were engaged in an all-out struggle against authoritarian and anti-social forces, a struggle which they won in 1945, on the Iberian peninsula the beginnings of an urban, progressive and cosmopolitan culture were swept aside in 1939 by the victory of a strongly atavistic, agrarian and reactionary Spain, still nostalgic for its imperial past. The great leap forward envisaged by the avant-garde was possible only for the few. After the Civil War, Franco's Spain reverted to the worst sort of backwardness. While the Europe beyond the Pyrenees set about making a new start, Spain marked time.

A demonstration outside the Palau de la Generalitat. On 2nd August 1931, the Catalans displayed once more their will to self-determination. In a plebiscite, the overwhelming majority voted for autonomy.
In 1934, the Generalitat in Barcelona proclaimed Catalan independence. However the central authorities in Madrid hit back, and numerous advocates of autonomy were arrested. Proudly the Guardia Civil displays the weapons confiscated after the insurrection of the night of 6th / 7th October 1934.

METROPOLITANO

Following double page:
Entrance hall and ticket office of the
"Gran Metro" in 1924 (above left, below
right); Arc del Triomf station on the "Metro
Transversal" line (below left), and Plaça de
Catalunya station (above right).

In 1926 Buïgas and his colleagues designed the Jaume I and Sant Sebastià
towers for a cable railway which was to
convey visitors to the 1929 World Exhibition from the docks to Montjuïc and back.
However, private money came only in a
trickle and, as a result, the project was
only completed – under Roda's direction –
in 1931, by which time the Exhibition had
already closed.

Planning for the World Exhibition also
went hand-in-hand with the construction
of an underground railway. The "Metro
Transversal", a line running parallel to the
shore, was followed by the "Gran Metro"
along the axis of the Passeig de Gràcia.
The picture, taken in 1925, shows municipal representatives on a fact-finding visit,
seeing for themselves how work was pro-
gressing at the Plaça de Catalunya.

As early as 1907 there were efforts on the part of leading Barcelona businessmen to stage another World Exhibition in the city. The projected date was 1914 and the venue was to be a site on the Montjuïc. In the course of preparations other considerations came to the fore and the original plan was replaced by one for an International Fair devoted specifically to the electrical industry, along with an exhibition of Spanish arts and crafts, to be held in 1916. This project suffered repeated postponements. When Primo de Rivera established his military dictatorship in Madrid in 1921, the plan underwent further radical changes. Josep Puig i Cadafalch, who was responsible for the general plan of the

Exposició d'Indústries Elèctriques, was declared persona non grata overnight. In addition, Rivera ordered a broadening of the theme: the World Exhibition was to represent the areas of industry, sport and Spanish art in equal measure. The definitive opening date was fixed for 19th May 1929. Two free-standing towers on the Plaça d'Espanya, reminiscent of Italian campanili, form the entrance to the route leading up to the Palau Nacional, the main building of the 1929 Exhibition. An attraction of the long connecting axis, the Avinguda Reina Maria Christina, is the "Magic Fountain" designed by Carles Buïgas, a synaesthetic play of music, light, colour and water in the style of Art Déco.

PALAU NACIONAL

Enric Català i Català, Pedro Cendoya Oscoz,
Pere Domènech i Roura, 1925–1929;
Gae Aulenti, Enric Steegmann, 1985–1992
Plaça del Mirador

Axonometric drawing of the main elements of the project.

The Palau Nacional was converted in
1934 into the Museu d'Art de Catalunya,
and from the mid-1980s underwent extensive restoration at the hands of the cele-
brated Italian architect, Gae Aulenti. As in
her conversion of the Gare d'Orsay in
Paris, her new museum concept is dominated by dominant, clearly structured built-
in elements.

PLAÇA DE L'UNIVERS

Jean Claude Nicolas Forestier, 1914–1922;
Pep Bonet, 1983–1985
Exhibition site on the Montjuïc

The Plaça de l'Univers, which dates back to Forestier's plans for the 1929 World Exhibition site, did not retain its Art Déco charm for long. The complex degenerated during the 1960s in particular, when buildings important for the spatial integrity of the square were demolished and replaced by structures that followed quite different criteria.

Bonet's restoration was based essentially on two elements: the building of new exhibition halls arranged in series and the uniform closure of the square's frontage by extending the façades. Cupolas over the entrances recall the original Art Déco design. Before it was placed at the square's centre, Josep Llimona's statue, "El Forjador" ("The Blacksmith"), dating from 1914, stood outside the Municipal Pavilion during the World Exhibition.

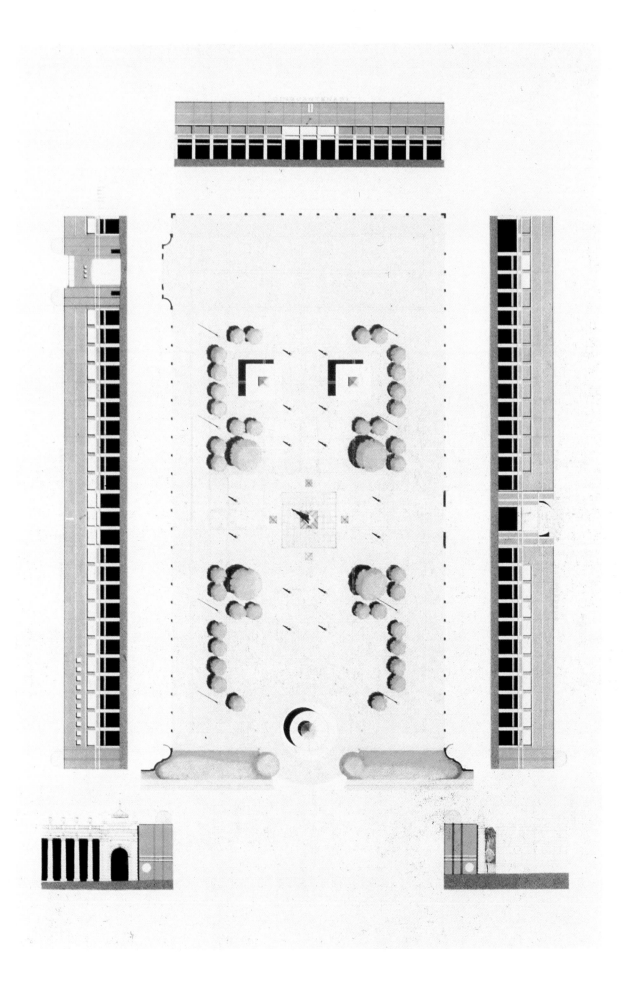

PALAU DE LES ARTS GRAFIQUES

Pelagi Martínez i Paricio, 1927–1929;
José Llinàs, 1984–1989
Carrer del Lleida

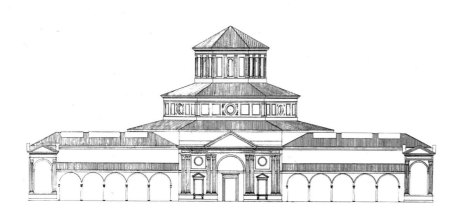

Many of the 1929 Exhibition pavilions, though intended only for temporary use, have been preserved right up to the present day. As happened with some of the buildings of the 1888 World Exhibition, some now house museum collections. This is also true of the former "Palace of Graphic Arts", an example of Noucentismo work by Pelagi Martínez, who re-interprets the Italian Renaissance; since 1932 it has been the home of the Archaeological Museum. José Llinàs' restoration, with its effective display ideas, goes back to the original spatial concept.

GERMAN STATE PAVILION

Ludwig Mies van der Rohe, 1929
Avinguda del Marquès de Comillas

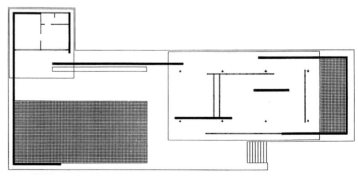

Ludwig Mies van der Rohe's pavilion was
the venue for the official opening of the
1929 Barcelona World Exhibition by King
Alfonso XIII of Spain – in the foreground,
left – and Queen Victoria Eugenia – in the
background, with the architect. In its light,
generously proportioned elegance, it was
far more than just a prestigious building.
In front of the long, flat-roofed structure
was a broad travertine terrace with a shallow pool, which successfully set the building off from the street. Wall planes, faced
in costly marble and metal-framed sheets
of glass in white, grey and green tints gave
structure to the flowing spatial continuum,
which – by dint of the clever placement of
openings – appeared extremely spacious
from the outside. The American critic
Helen Appleton Read summarized her re-
port on the World Exhibition as follows:
"Among the nations represented, only Germany made her modern industrial and cultural status symbolically clear... The austerely elegant pavilion by Mies van der
Rohe, a pioneer of modern architecture, is
a symbol of this country's post-war culture, a convincing presentation of modern
architectural aesthetics... He is a radical
rationalist and his designs are governed by
a passion for beautiful architecture. Mies
is one of the few modern architects whose
theory transcends sterile functional for-
mulas and is thereby transformed into artistic design. The means whereby he
achieves this impression of elegant se-
renity are his materials and his spatial conception." At the time, the pavilion stood
for just a few months; a faithful replica
was constructed on the same site in 1985
by Cristià Cirici, Ferran Ramos and Ignasi
de Solà-Morales.

MYRURGIA FACTORY

Antoni Puig i Gairalt, 1928–1930
Carrer de Mallorca 351

Antoni Puig's two-storey factory won the
City of Barcelona Prize for the best building of the year as soon as it was completed. The façades of the building – a rec-
tangle with two truncated corners – are
dominated by the factory's strip windows.
The vertical entrance porch seems in a
sense to be standing in defiance of the
horizontal structure behind it. Behind
three elaborately decorated glass doors is
the foyer, where the visitor is confronted
by an elegant staircase somewhat reminiscent of Art Déco – reticent and imposing
at the same time. A perfume factory, it is
one of the best examples of rationalist
architecture in a Catalonia which had left
Modernismo, Noucentismo and every
form of historicism behind it once and for
all and was now devoted to an architecture of straight lines and pure volumes.

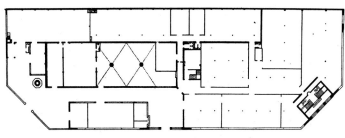

BARRAQUER CLINIC
Joaquim Lloret i Homs, 1934–1940
Carrer de Muntaner 314

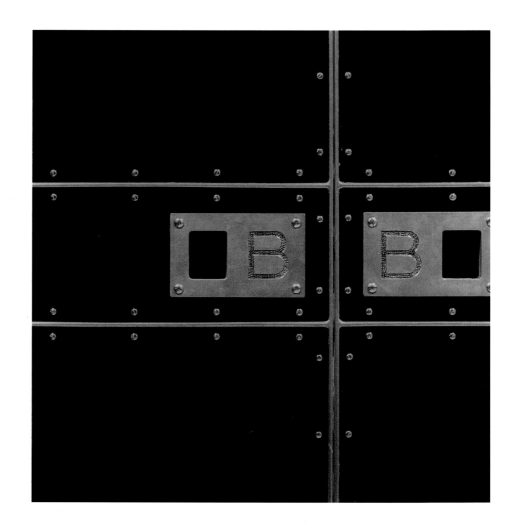

The eye-clinic run by the then well-known ocultist Dr. Barraquer on the corner of Carrer de Muntaner and Carrer de Laforia looks dynamically smooth from the outside, reminiscent of buildings by Erich Mendelsohn or the brothers Hans and Wassili Luckhardt. In contrast, the interior is a highly individual mixture of functionalism, with a great deal of attention to detail, and set-pieces borrowing on the repertoire of forms characteristic of Art Déco: details of door (above left, below right), reception (below left), operating theatre (above right).

APARTMENT BLOCK (left)

Josep Lluís Sert i López, 1930–1931
Carrer de Muntaner 342–348

TUBERCULOSIS CLINIC

Josep Lluís Sert i López, Josep Torres i Clavé,
Joan B. Subirana i Subirana, 1934–1938
Passatge de Sant Bernat 10

The apartment block on the Carrer de
Muntaner was Lluís Sert's first important
commission. He had previously collaborated for a year with Le Corbusier. This
building is reckoned among the most successful examples of Spanish Rationalism.
Each apartment extends over two storeys;
the corner of the building is given plastic
emphasis by means of projecting elements
and small balconies.
The tuberculosis clinic was commissioned
by the Catalan regional government; it is
one of the few projects the GATCPAC
architects managed to carry out.
The GATCPAC had practically no time in
which to realize its plans. Founded at a
fairly late stage, in 1930, by which point
the avant-garde had already established itself in many European countries, its activities came to a sudden end with the outbreak of the Spanish Civil War in 1936.
Josep Torres was killed in action in 1939.
Together with Lluís Sert, he had been the
group's driving force. Sert emigrated via
Paris to the USA, where he became Dean
and Walter Gropius' successor at Harvard.

CASA BLOC
GATCPAC, 1932–1936
Passeig de Torras i Bages 91–105

The purpose behind the Casa Bloc estate was actually to provide affordable housing for working-class families. However, the GATCPAC was never in a position to put the complex to its intended use. When Franco's troops occupied Barcelona towards the end of the Civil War, the apartments were confiscated for use by police personnel. Although planned for low-income families, the apartments are not short on comfort. They are all south-facing and the number of rooms per flat is flexible, as a result of the maisonette design. The neighbouring site was used for the prototypes of Casa Bloc. There, as in Casa Bloc itself, important elements of the great design to replan Barcelona are discernible, a design in whose early stages Le Corbusier also had a hand. His theory of social housing coincided with the committed social policies of Catalonia's first president, Macià.

V

FROM THE END OF THE CIVIL WAR
TO THE CONSUMER SOCIETY

The Fémina, one of Barcelona's first large cinemas, underwent a major restoration programme between 1949 and 1951. As a result of the comprehensive rebuilding measures, two entirely separate auditoria with a common screen were created. The gallery was only accessible from the Carrer de la Diputació, while the stalls could only be reached from the Passeig de Gràcia. A conspicuous feature is the undulating wood cladding of the new façade.

The end of the Civil War led to the dissolution of the GATCPAC. Josep Torres i Clavé had been killed in action and most of the members went into exile in America. Some remained in Barcelona waiting to see how events would turn out, while some of the émigrés gradually returned. Josep Lluís Sert, who had worked together with Le Corbusier, became one of the leading lights of the Modern Movement. As President, from 1947 to 1956, of the International Congress of Modern Architecture (Congrès Internationale d'Architecture Moderne – CIAM), he was one of the major advocates of the new, rationalist principles. He settled in Harvard, producing much remarkable architecture in the United States. Years later he returned to Barcelona, where his Les Escales Park residential complex in Pedralbes (1973–1976), and his Joan-Miró-Foundation in the Parc de Montjuïc (1972–1974) constituted a significant breakthrough for the Modern Movement.

Another of the young architects to emigrate to America, Antoni Bonet i Castellana, was to become one of the most important harbingers of modern architecture in Argentina and Uruguay. Like Sert before him, he realized a number of projects in Barcelona and the surrounding area during the 1950s, for example, the Casa la Ricarda in Prat de Llobregat (1953–1960). In 1963 he returned for good to Barcelona, where in the 1960s he designed two very interesting buildings: the Edificio Mediterrani (1960–1966) on the Carrer del Consell de Cent, which re-interpreted, from a modern point of view, the apartment house of the Eixample, and the Meridiana greyhound track (1962–1963), with its elegantly rounded steel roof, and the striking sunshade suspended from it.[32]

But even before the return of these pre-war masters to Barcelona there were young and eager talents who, in the late forties, were doing what they could to arouse Catalan architecture from the sluggishness and backwardness into which the Franco regime had forced it: the intervening years since the innovative period of the Second Spanish Republic had seen a return to stylistic Classicism and "monumental" city-planning.

Catalonia's peripheral location within Spain on the one hand and her proximity to France and Italy on the other, together with her own Mediterranean and rationalist tradition, all prepared the way for a new architecture in which international trends and native Catalan roots were blended. Not to be underestimated in this development is the role of such major architects as Alberto Sartoris (1949), Bruno Zevi (1950), Alvar Aalto (1951), Nikolaus Pevsner (1952), Gio Ponti (1953) and Alfred Roth (1955), who all visited Barcelona during this period, giving lectures which left a deep impression on the young architects of the region. Various projects dating from this period bear witness to the gradual

transformation: the Hotel Park (1950–1954) and the Fémina cinema (1951) by Antoni de Moragas,[33] the houses which José Antonio Coderch designed for Barceloneta (1952–1954), the Gustavo Gili publishing house by Francesc Bassó and Joaquim Gili (1954–1961), the houses on the Carrer de Pallars by Bohigas and Martorell (1958–1959), and the Casa M.M.I. (1955–1958) by Josep Maria Sostres. All these buildings demonstrate how formal patterns, valid the world over, were re-interpreted according to the individual "feel" of the architects concerned.

In order to promote this renewal of architecture and town planning, a number of young architects founded the "R" Group with the intention of encouraging exhibitions and competitions among students of architecture. Its models were Cerdà's Eixample plan, Catalan Modernismo and the Rationalism promoted by GATCPAC. At the same time, they tried to draw closer to international trends, especially the Neo-Liberty and Contextualism of Italy and the Organicism and Empiricism of the Nordic countries.

This resuscitation of architecture had its parallels in other disciplines. In art, it was manifested in the work of the "Dau al Set" group and in the appearance of various other groups concerned with literature and the cinema. These groups were united by their common membership in the "Escuela de Barcelona". It was during this period that José Antonio Coderch, a member of "Team 10" and the planner of such projects as the Casa Ugalde in Caldetes near Barcelona, emerged as the most outstanding of the Catalan architects. Without concealing the debt he owed to the architectural ideas and work of the time, such as those of Luis Barragán in Mexico, Fernando Távora in Portugal or Aldo van Eyck in Holland, Coderch developed spatial concepts that were all his own. In this, he managed to make do with a paucity of elements, an economy he had learned from the vernacular architecture of the Mediterranean region. His system underlines the privacy of the dwelling area, protecting it with walls and blinds. The living quarters consist of suites of large rooms, continually interrupted and placed around internal patios which cannot be seen from outside.[34]

The maturity and the renewal of Catalan architecture were reflected to a certain extent in the quality of the proposals put forward on the occasion of the competition for the new headquarters of the Collegi Oficial d'Arquitectes de Catalunya. It was Xavier Busquets who finally realized this so decidedly modern building in the middle of the Old City.

Once the "R" Group had attained its first objectives, it dissolved itself: by the early sixties, modern architecture had become established in Catalonia.[35] Many other young architects at that time were already turning towards a new, common

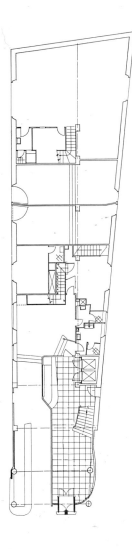

HOTEL PARK

Antoni de Moragas, 1950–1954
Avinguda del Marquès de l'Argentera 11

The importance of this work lies in the fact that it is the first document of modern architecture after the Civil War and the ten years of total mediocrity which followed. In this project, Moragas put ideas into practice which he had gleaned from professional journals and from visiting lecturers at the university's Department of Architecture. Especially important in this respect were the Scandinavians, Gunnar Asplund and Alvar Aalto, along with Dutch rationalists such as Johannes Duiker. Although the building is in the old city, Moragas succeeded in integrating the decidedly modern structure harmoniously into its surroundings. In 1990 the hotel underwent a total restoration (plan).

style. As the sixties drew to a close, Oriol Bohigas described this trend, in allusion to the names of other groups in the city, as the "Escuela de Barcelona".[36] A majority of the former members of the "R" Group continued to orient themselves towards the programme of this school. They were now joined by architects such as Federico Correa and Alfonso Milà, Lluís Cantallops, Lluís Domènech, Ramon Maria Puig, Leandre Sabater, Lluís Nadal, Vicenç Bonet, Pere Puigdefàbregas and the Studio PER. Their architecture followed the guidelines set by the so-called Realismo style. This concept, begun by the Roman Neo-Realists, such as Ludovico Quaroni, and continuing through to the Milanese theoreticians, such as Ernesto Nathan Rogers, had been espoused by numerous Italian architects. Among the projects scattered across the whole of Catalonia, the following are particularly noteworthy: the dwelling-houses built by Martorell-Bohigas-Mackay in the Avinguda de la Meridiana (1959–1965), the Edificio Monitor in the Avinguda Diagonal by Correa-Milà (1969–1970), and the student hostel, Mare Güell, designed by Cantallops-Rodrigo (1963–1967).

Taking a closer look at these buildings emanating from the "Escuela de Barcelona", one can clearly discern their distinguishing characteristics: the search for a compositional method which would define the whole by the individual parts; the use of a style which gives expression to the clarity of constructive logic and which brings out the quality of the craftsmanship as well as of the materials employed, such as brick or ceramics – so important in traditional Catalan architecture – and thus conducive both to communicative and to didactic objectives; the careful planning of connecting spaces, such as entrances, courtyards and stairwells; and a commitment to the educational and communicative role of architecture as a medium between building culture and user. This architecture, deeply rooted as it is in Catalan culture, was characterized by the typical Catalan blend of realism, empiricism and pragmatism.[37]

The architects Enric Tous and Josep Maria Fargas struck out on a path which diverged from that of the "Escuela de Barcelona". They advocated an even more thorough application of the technological possibilities available. With the Banca Catalana (1965–1968), an office block constructed from pre-fabricated components, they succeeded in placing a new, carefully conceived, prestigious building on a site so demanding of sensitive treatment as the Passeig de Gràcia. At almost exactly the same time, the internationally renowned team of Belgiojoso-Peressutti-Rogers built the headquarters of the Spanish subsidiary of the Olivetti corporation (1960–1964), likewise in the city centre, on the Ronda Universidad. The Milan team decided on a glass curtain façade right in the middle of historic Barcelona.

CITROËN BRANCH HEADQUARTERS

The most important building in this context, however, is without doubt Josep Maria Sostres' office block for the newspaper *Noticiero Universal* (1963–1965). If Gaudí's Casa Milà set the standard for architectural exuberance within Cerdà's grid, the *Noticiero Universal* building represents the border to Minimalism and Abstraction. Sostres interprets the logic of the Eixample façades with great precision as a smooth plane, a skin which separates the internal rooms from the public space of the street. Conspicuous within this plane are the vertical outlines – typical of the historical Eixample – of the balconies. To enhance the sense of modern abstraction still further, he eschewed any ledges at the ends of the gables.

While a few talented architects were constructing rather small, but exemplary buildings, the 1960s' economic boom saw an increase in population density resulting from an architecture which served purely speculative ends, an architecture which filled up every possible plot of land, left no room for green open spaces and spread like some oil-slick towards the adjacent villages and the surrounding countryside. The Eixample saw for the first time planning permission given for penthouse flats, which seriously spoiled the volumetric unity of the apartment blocks. The general building fever even led to the demolition of some Modernismo buildings – Modernismo being out of favour at the time. In the suburbs, the policy pursued was a bloodless and speculative version of rationalistic town planning. Satellite towns sprang up, which were in truth nothing but a cheap imitation of the French "Grandes Ensembles", an architecture of poor quality which deprived its inhabitants of any infrastructure.

At the same time, the ravages of the tourist industry were despoiling the Catalan coast of its rural character. As if it were not enough for the Franco regime to have left the marks of its repressive nature on the generations fron the 1930s and 1940s, it now began to force through urban development at any price. The result was a legacy, still with us today, of faceless towns and rural areas without any character or tradition.

Even so, culturally worthwhile architecture did not stagnate. During the 1960s, some Barcelona architects were designing buildings which demonstrated that a clear break had been made with the tradition of the "Escuela de Barcelona". Thus in 1963 Ricardo Bofill founded the Taller de Arquitectura, an architecture workshop, which, following a few early works in the style of the "Escuela", began to advocate an experimental spatial design oriented towards the new technological trends being propagated by, among others, the British group Archigram. Bofill's experiments reached their climax in the Walden 7 apartment complex in Sant Just Desvern (1970–1975): a kind of city in space, albeit built with conventional technology.

APARTMENT BLOCK (left)

José Antonio Coderch de Sentmenat,
Manuel Valls i Vergés, 1951–1954
Passeig Nacional 43

WORKS HOUSING ESTATE

Oriol Bohigas, Josep Maria Martorell,
1958–1959
Carrer de Pallars 299–317

Coderch is the outstanding Catalan architect of the second half of the 20th century. This apartment block became the symbol of the rebirth of modern architecture in Barcelona. The work is characterized by introverted rooms flowing into one another, protected from the outside by wooden Venetian blinds. The juxtaposition of clear, modern forms with conventional elements is a distinguishing and rather startling feature of this building. Bohigas and Martorell decided on craft-based construction techniques and traditional materials, which accord more closely with the given situation and with the taste of the times.

With clear references to the work of American architect Robert Venturi, the young team at the Studio PER – Lluís Clotet, Oscar Tusquets, Christian Cirici and Pep Bonet – were also designing evocative, communicative architecture, post-modern in character. One example is the extension to an apartment house on the Carrer de Sant Màrius, an expressive collage of mass-produced building materials, executed by Clotet and Tusquets between 1969 and 1971.

Finally, Albert Viaplana and Helio Piñón found a conceptual and abstract solution for the architecture of the late 20th century, a solution closely related to the ideas of the Americans, Peter Eisenman and John Hejduk. A period of silent and patient experimentation was followed in the early eighties by their much-discussed design for the rebuilding of the Plaça dels Països Catalans in front of Sants railway station.[38]

To sum up, one can say that Barcelona's architecture during the 1970s reflected the various new methodologies, exemplified worldwide, of Aldo Rossi, Robert Venturi and Peter Eisenman.

During this period, José Antonio Coderch made a captivating impact both through his severity and through his ability to achieve particularly impressive results with the use of few formal means. At that time, it was Coderch who set the standard for modern architecture in Barcelona. Among his works were the Trade office towers (1966–1969) in the city's commercial centre, with their glazed, uniquely rounded shape, as well as the Urquijo Bank's residential complex in the Carrer Raset (1967), one of the most perfect achievements in the whole area of residential estates. His Institut Français (1972–1975), a bare, cubic structure, assuredly deserves a mention here, as does his posthumous (he had died in 1984) extension to the Escuela de Arquitectura de Barcelona (1978–1985), a low pavilion, which serves as a base to the existing high-rise building. Thus did Coderch prove his ability to make quite personal architectural statements.

Alongside of those already mentioned, there are other excellent buildings dating from the 1970s, such as the apartment block on the Passeig de la Bonanova (1970–1973) by Martorell-Bohigas-Mackay or the Edificio Frégoli (1972–1975) by Esteve Bonell. These already give a hint of the diffuse but elegant eclecticism which was to spread through Catalan architecture during the 1980s.[39]

COLLEGI OFICIAL D'ARQUITECTES DE CATALUNYA

Xavier Busquets i Sindreu, 1958–1962
Plaça Nova 5

In 1957 a competition was held for the design of a new building for the Collegi Oficial d'Arquitectes de Catalunya. It turned out to be a testament to the maturity of Catalan architecture. What was wanted was a decidedly modern structure for a site in the heart of the old city, opposite the cathedral. The competition, to which entries were submitted by the most able architects of the time, was won by Xavier Busquets.

Before the project could be implemented, however, major alterations had to be made to the original concept. The solution, as finally realized, consisted of a horizontal structure with a glass façade on the ground floor – the exhibition room – and a totally self-contained structure on the first floor, the hall. Above it looms the high-rise block, used for administration, teaching and research. The smooth inner and outer walls of the hall are decorated with a chiselled mural designed by Pablo Picasso.

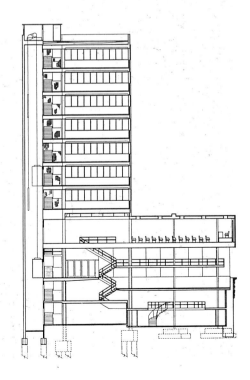

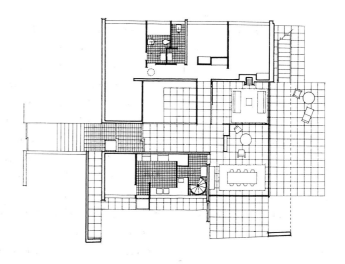

CASA M. M. I.

Josep Maria Sostres i Maluquer, 1955–1958
Ciutat Diagonal

Among all the architects who acted as driving forces in the movement for architectural renewal, Josep Maria Sostres is among the most open-minded and willing to experiment. The variety of architectural forms which he employed in his designs – in the mountains, by the sea and in the city – is proof of this, if any were needed. The Casa M. M. I., with its horizontal structure and clear lines, is an outstanding example of his indefatigable search for an architecture in tune with the times.

The house looks different from every side: to the north, it is closed, being open to the garden on the south side. Between the bedrooms and bathrooms on the one hand, and the working area with its kitchen and study on the other, are the inner courtyard, the living-room, the dining-room and the terrace. A spiral staircase connects the garage with the study and with the glass pavilion on the roof terrace. From the narrow staircase at the entrance, the visitor proceeds to rooms that become ever more spacious and brighter, until he arrives on the open terrace. The porch and the long blind above the glass frontage to the south form a kind of second skin, which keeps the house cool in summer; additional fresh air is provided by the patio.

Light and shade, glossy and matt surfaces, dark and light hues – these are the chief organizers of space, their reflections, contrasts and shimmering light conjuring up ever new geometric figures and shadow effects.

GUSTAVO GILI PUBLISHING HOUSE

Francesc Bassó i Birulés, Joaquim Gili
i Moros, 1954–1961
Carrer del Rosselló 89

Situated in the open space within one of Cerdà's blocks, this publishing house is an outstanding example of modern architecture designed for the world of work, making clear allusions to the masterpieces of the International Style of the 1930s.

The interior radiates a distinctly functional atmosphere and is devoid of any decorative elements. The large open-plan offices take up two levels on the ground and mezzanine floors of the main building. No less reticent and cool is the colour plan, which is restricted to black, white and grey.

The main façade has a gigantic slatted sunblind of projecting concrete. For the rest, the picture is characterized – totally in keeping with the example of classical modern architecture – by smoothly plastered surfaces, pilotis and steel-framed strip windows.

SEAT PREMISES

César Ortiz Echagüe, Rafael Echaide Itarte,
1958–1960
Plaça d'Ildefons Cerdà, Passeig de la Zona
Franca 270, Gran Via de les Corts
Catalanes 140; Dependance

HOUSING ESTATE

Oriol Bohigas, Josep Maria Martorell,
David Mackay, 1959–1965
Avinguda de la Meridiana 312–316

HOUSING ESTATE

José Antonio Coderch, Manuel Valls,
1957–1961
Carrer de Johann Sebastian Bach 7

Once modern architecture had become established in Catalonia, Bohigas, Martorell and Mackay felt free – with their work on the Avinguda de la Meridiana, which they conceived as a manifesto – to express their opposition to the speculative tendencies which were becoming apparent on the Barcelona building scene. The floor plans of the individual apartments are relatively generous in their proportions; the façade has taken on the function of a protective rampart and its numerous small windows are reminiscent of a beehive. Each individual window is oriented in such a way that it shields the apartment in the most effective way possible against the background of traffic noise from the broad street outside.

While Coderch, Sostres, Bassó and Gili followed the models of Le Corbusier, Mies van der Rohe, Alvar Aalto or Richard Neutra, the architectural style of Bohigas, Martorell and Mackay was more in tune with the craft-based brick structures of the Amsterdam school, as represented, for example, by Michel de Kerk, Pieter Lodewijk Kramer or Hendricus Theodorus Wijdeveld.

The façade of the apartment block on the Carrer de Johann Sebastian Bach is dominated, as was already the case in Coderch's building on the Passeig Nacional in Barceloneta, by large Venetian blinds. The internal organization is similar to that in Gaudí's Casa Milà: access to the individual apartments is not by means of a staircase, but by a lift directly to the apartment. All the rooms in an apartment are oriented towards this central entry.

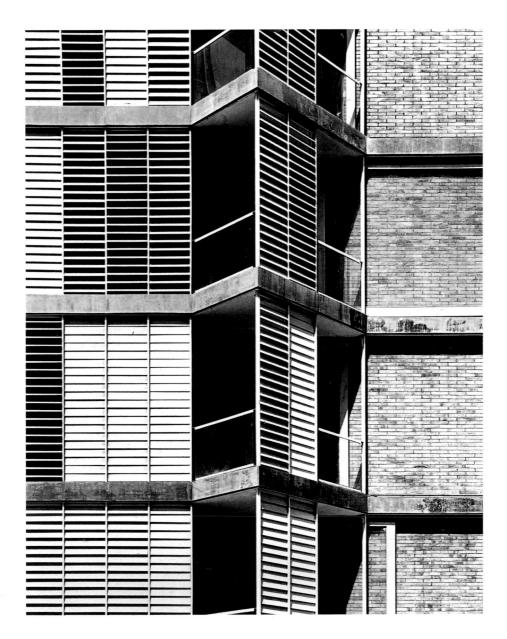

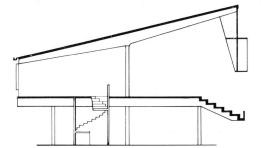

The specification was clear – a greyhound track with grandstand and betting counters – and the architectural response was striking. The building stretches along the finishing straight. The terraces, at the curved rear of which are the betting counters, lie well above the arena, permitting an unobstructed view of the proceedings. Geometrically speaking, the roof describes a very gentle arc, truncated at each end. The gaping opening between the horizontal line of the grandstand and the obliquely placed roof – from which a large slatted sun blind is suspended – is reminiscent of a long, half-open oyster. The filigree steel structure gives the ensemble, which seems to nestle almost playfully up to the arena, an air of lightness and elegance.

FUNDACIO JOAN MIRO

Sert, Jackson and Associates, 1972–1974;
Jaume Freixa i Janáriz, 1988
Parc de Montjuïc, Avinguda de Miramar

The foundation, set up privately by Joan Miró in 1971, had basically two aims. One, of course, was to provide a worthy setting for the works of this Catalan artist in a permanent home. This was made possible by substantial donations, supplemented by changing temporary exhibitions on particular themes in his œuvre. The other aim was the general encouragement of contemporary art at an international level.

The design of the Joan Miró Foundation is due to Josep Lluís Sert, a close friend of the artist. It is one of the few outstanding works of modern architecture in Barcelona of supra-regional importance.

Sert took up the approach adopted by Le Corbusier, employing the idea of a spiral museum layout, permitting further extension at any time. The soft, refracted light which imbues the exhibition rooms was achieved by means of a decidedly horizontal layout for the whole complex. The extensive roofscape which this necessitated is convincingly employed to display Miró's sculptures. Jaume Freixa's extension follows the design concept of the main building.

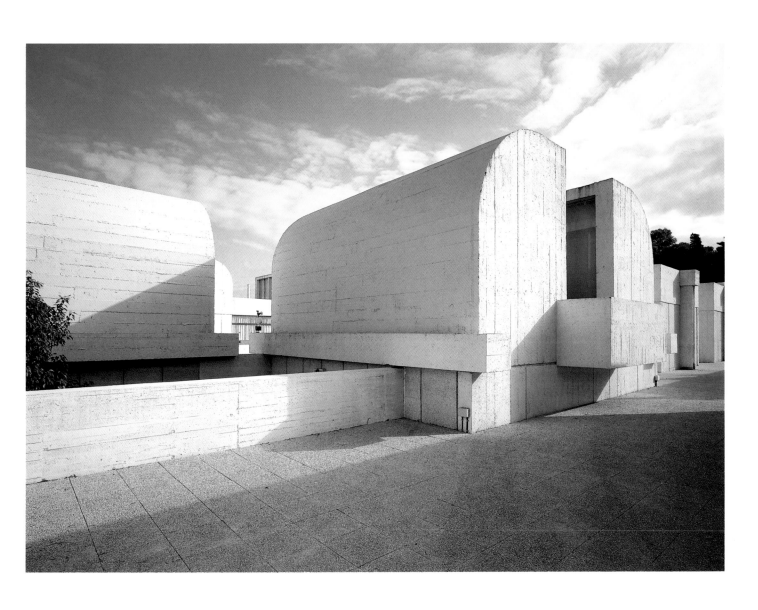

WALDEN 7

Ricardo Bofill, Taller de Arquitectura,
1970–1975
Sant Just Desvern

This massive residential block, consisting
of 400 standardized "dwelling cubes" materialized after comprehensive theoretical
preliminary work among the members of
Bofill's team, the Taller de Arquitectura, an
architectural workshop which had set up
its offices in the immediate vicinity of an
abandoned cement factory. Under the influence of the technological utopias of the
1960s, the intention was to try out alternatives to conventional urban structures, in
the shape of a formalization of the urban
setting in space. The plan was for a vertical city, based on communicative links between individual accommodation units
with communal facilities. It was conceived
for big-city people, liberated from all traditional social conventions, seeking new
styles of living. The experiment was a
failure; the complex is currently in a
ruinous condition.

235

VI

BARCELONA TODAY

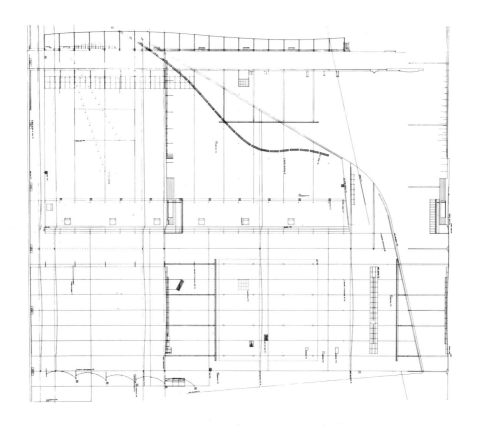

As the 1970s drew to a close, Barcelona made a first attempt to rid itself of the disastrous town-planning legacy of the Franco era. During the transitional phase of democratization at the local government level, preliminary steps had already been taken by the Mayor, Josep Maria Socias (1976–1979), under the planning direction of architect Josep Antoni Solans, to make available publicly-owned plots of land, to promote social programmes such as the building of low-cost flats and the creation of public open spaces, and to convey buildings of historical interest back into municipal ownership. These developments were given major impetus by the Socialist-led city council (since 1979), at first under Narcís Serra and, from 1982, under Pasqual Maragall.

In the early 1980s, the architect and town-planning commissioner, Oriol Bohigas, was taken on to advise on all municipal initiatives. The result was a slowly maturing modernization plan, which took into account the specific features and basic characteristics of the city. Barcelona was to be renewed and restructured; public buildings and squares were once again to become the hallmark of each individual district. Even then, there was already speculation as to the possibility of winning the nomination for the 1992 Olympics. The assumption was that the synthesis of town-planning ideas and the special requirements of an Olympic venue would make possible a completely new and comprehensive approach to the whole restructuring project.[40]

The building projects of this period were directed primarily towards creating public parks and squares and towards the establishment of community centres in numerous districts of the city. Thought was also already being given to the erection of new stadia, swimming-pools and the like: thus 1983 saw the announcement of the competition for the Anell Olímpic, the Olympic Ring, and the new cycle track in the Horta district was inaugurated.

In October 1986, the city's hopes were fulfilled: Barcelona was to be the venue for the 1992 Olympic Games. The positive aspect of this development was that a wish harboured by the city since 1932 had at last come true; that was the year, namely, when Barcelona had bid unsuccessfully against Berlin to stage the 1936 Games. The other side of the coin was that time was short: the city had to rethink practically her entire infrastructure; the required buildings meant the city was put under considerable pressure, and for the citizens, this pressure meant that everyday life became more and more expensive.[41]

Building measures since 1986 have differed from their predecessors in a number of respects: extent, cost, deadline, specification and client. Every project has had to be planned and officially approved as quickly as possible. Citizens' action groups have had to take a back seat, and the city, a sensitive organism that can

PLAÇA DELS PAÏSOS CATALANS
Helio Piñón, Albert Viaplana, Enric Miralles, 1981–1983
Carrer de Muntades

The square beside the Sants railway station is one of a number of squares laid out by the Barcelona city council during the course of the 1980s. It illustrates the new trend towards an intellectual architecture which aims for formal abstraction. The gently undulating surface of the square is scattered with geometric figures, sculptures, colonnades, forms and elements taken from the repertoire of architecture, the expressive possibilities of the architect and the magic reality of the plan on the drawing-board.

Following double page:

PLAÇA DEL SOL (above left)
Jaume Bach, Gabriel Mora, 1981–1985

PARC DE L'ESPANYA INDUSTRIAL (below left and above right)
Lluís Peña Ganchegui, Francesc Rius, 1981–1986

PEU DEL FUNICULAR DE VALLVIDRERA (below right)
José Llinàs, 1982–1985
Avinguda de Vallvidrera, Carrer de Carrós

only grow when all have a part to play, has had to close ranks in a race against time. It has had to eliminate the consultation process to a dangerous extent rather than act out its role, in Franco Rellas' words, "as the venue par excellence for argument and conflict, the last space in which it is possible to carry on a dialogue with truth through a constant confrontation of ideas."[42]

To sum up, it can be said that Barcelona's growth since the 1980s has been determined by two factors: the first is the attempt by the democratically elected council to make up for lost time in the matter of infrastructure development; the other is the opportunity presented by the Olympic Games to mobilize investments and channel them in a particular direction.

Current building measures are subject to the stipulation that they should complement the city in its existing form. Large plots which have become vacant through the clearance of obsolete infrastructure – for example, railway stations and tracks, factories, and former hospitals – are being redeveloped, new open spaces created, specified districts replanned for traffic, and the whole street network upgraded. As a large part of Barcelona is already fixed in its structure, the most drastic changes are being made not in the centre, but on the periphery, in other words, in the suburbs, along the main entry and exit routes, along the coastal strip and on the mountain slopes.[43]

Individual intrusions into the existing structure should of course complement this structure and improve it; in some cases, though, the interference has been drastic, changing the city to its disadvantage. The addition of small construction details, so typical of Barcelona, has been neglected in the process. This is also true to a certain extent of the Anell Olímpic competition complex and of the Vila Olímpica, the Olympic Village. Formally, the most recent building activities fall into four groups: areas, lines, junctions and points. "Areas" refers to the four city venues for Olympic Games events in 1992. The most important project is the construction of the Olympic Village: not only will an important section of the coastal strip thereby be brought back into use, at the same time an entirely new residential district will also be created. Barcelona, which has always sought to extend itself westwards, is now attempting to break with this long outdated tradition (common to all towns and cities, according to Claude Lévi-Strauss[44]) and to shift its direction of growth to the east.

The solution which has been found for the Olympic Village, however, provides no cause for any great expectations, for it remains limited in its scope and practical application. It contains none of the characteristic features of Cerdà's plan, nor does it make use of any of the benefits of modern town planning or of the typological categories that would arise from a precise division of the indi-

NEW BOTANICAL GARDENS

Carlos Ferrater, Josep Lluís Canosa,
Beth Figueras, 1988
Montjuïc

This project is still in the planning stage
and is one of the most innovative in the recent history of Barcelona architecture. The
central feature of the Gardens is a building
complex whose two wings are connected
to each other by a bridge-like structure.
The complex integrates a number of different spheres: museum, hot-houses, herba-
rium, research facilities, restaurant, offices.
The site, with its large variety of Mediterranean flora, is criss-crossed by a network
of paths whose structure is based on the
Mandelbrot model.

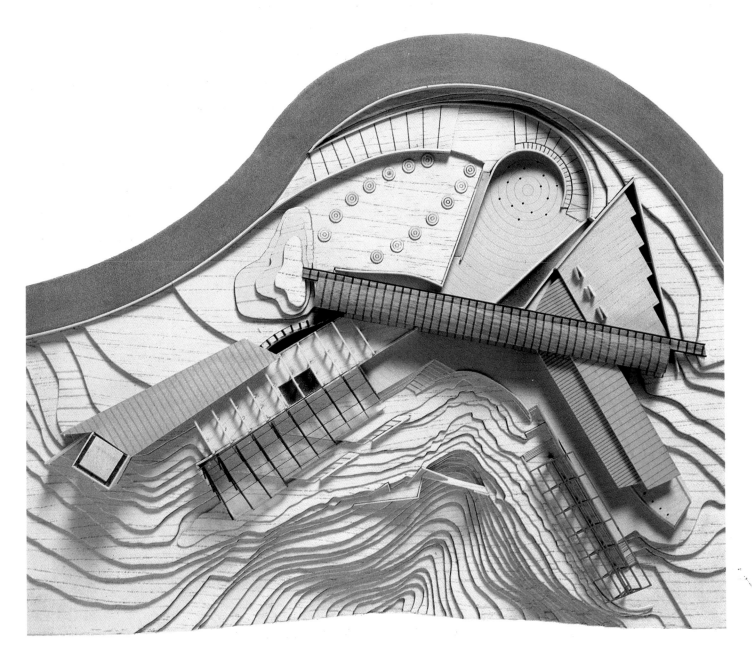

vidual measures and responsibilities. The most striking elements of the Olympic Village are two almost identical skyscrapers, one of which was designed by the Chicago firm of Skidmore, Owings & Merrill.[45]

Greater coherence of form and better spatial division can be seen in the project realized by a team led by Carlos Ferrater, covering three blocks of the Cerdà plan (1988–1992). Ferrater is one of those Catalan architects who have succeeded in developing an individual and especially precise method and form of expression. In the case of the project in question, the blocks as single units have been broken up to make room for avenues and to erect conspicuous towers at every corner. In addition, the interior gardens represent a new interpretation of Cerdà's original idea.[46]

An eye-catching building in the Vall d'Hebron, which took shape at an early stage in the current redevelopment, is the cycle track in Horta, mentioned above, by Esteve Bonell and Francesc Rius. Other sporting venues, both indoor and open-air, include the archery range, designed by Enric Miralles and Carme Pinós (1989–1992).

The most important Olympic site is the Anell Olímpic on Montjuïc, Barcelona's local hill. The complex stands on an enormous platform and embraces four major sporting venues: the Olympic Stadium, the Palau Sant Jordi Olympic indoor arena, the Instituto Nacional de Educación Física (College of Physical Education) and the Picornell baths. The most striking of these buildings is the Palau Sant Jordi, designed by a team led by Japanese architect Arata Isozaki (1984–1990). It resembles a sculptured shell resting on a cubic base. The façade facing the Anell Olímpic combines transparency with volumetric form, thus giving the building a monumental character which thereby indulges the fancy of the inhabitants for being entranced by edifices of enormous scale.[47]

With respect to the "lines" in our list, there is no doubt whatever that adequate connections between all the city districts and the Olympic venues can only be guaranteed if the necessary infrastructure – ring-roads, boulevards, bridges, tunnel and subway lines – are upgraded and extended. In order to achieve this goal, an attempt has been made to put into practice a new rapid-transit concept adapted to the city's requirements and at the same time providing park-like facilities for pedestrians.

The communications system is being completed by two further buildings. One is the Telecommunications Tower in Collserola, designed by Norman Foster (1989–1992), which gathers into one single technological unit all the aerials hitherto scattered about the hills and stands out against the skyline as a sort of symbolic monument to the technology which it embodies. The other is the new

PARC DE L'ESTACIO DEL NORD

Andreu Arriola, Carme Fiol, Enric Pericas, 1985–1987

Here, the wasteland adjacent to the old, disused North Station was exploited to lay out a park. It forms the starting-point for a large-scale "green concept" along the tracks as far as the Plaça del General Moragues and the Parc Sant Marti.
The park is laid out around two large works by the American sculptor Beverly Pepper. One of these, entitled "Cel Caigut" ("Pale Sky"), seems to grow out of the terrain and is reminiscent of a stranded whale; the other, entitled "Espiral Abrada", consists of wooden spirals planted with trees.

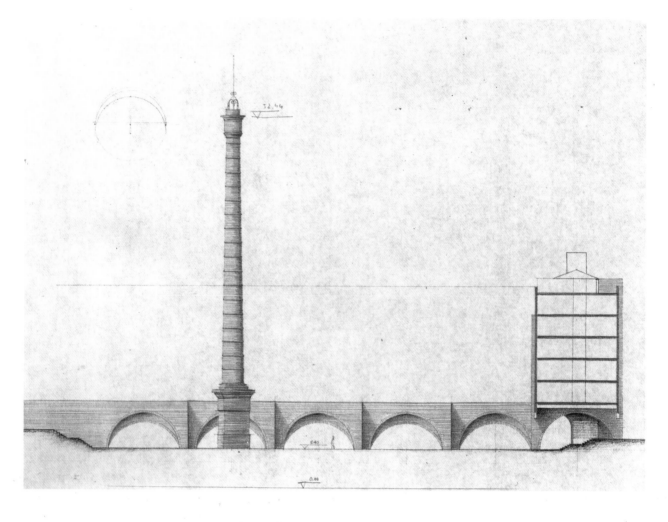

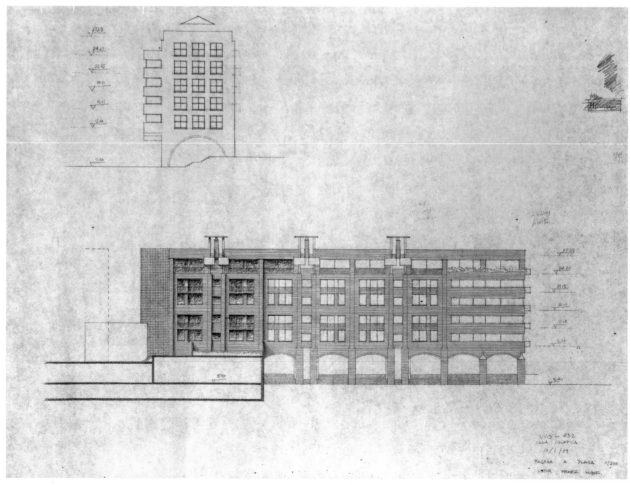

Barcelona Airport designed by Ricardo Bofill and his team (1987–1991), a linear conception with terminals on a triangular ground plan. They are placed along a covered avenue with double-glazed façades. In addition, the city's traffic network has been enriched by a particularly sculptural element, namely the bridge between Bach de Roda and Felip II streets (1986–1987), built of steel and reinforced concrete to a design by Santiago Calatrava.[48]

The "junctions" within the complex urban structure mediate between areas and are situated in the boundary strips between the individual districts, or else appear where various channels of communication meet. These "junctions" are represented by, for example, the reshaping of Port Vell, or else the concentration of high-rise office blocks in the Carrer Tarragona. Another such "junction" is the complex of open spaces, sports facilities and commercial premises on the Renfe Meridiana. New urban spaces like these, arising from the disappearance of obsolete infrastructural elements, today constitute major planning fields.[49]

A hitherto unsolved problem is the utilization of one of the city's most important "junctions", namely the Plaça de les Glòries Catalanes, which is still giving rise to a host of questions. Two projected buildings are intended to contribute to the vitalization of the square: the Teatre Nacional de Catalunya by Ricardo Bofill and Rafael Moneo's Auditorio Municipal. Finally, among the "selective" additions, we should mention the parks and squares which enjoy the particular favour of Barcelona's current municipal policymakers and already number about a hundred. Some of these varied projects are of a pioneering character, such as the Plaça dels Països Catalans in Sants, designed by Albert Viaplana, Helio Piñón and Enric Miralles (1981–1983), a manifesto of conceptual architecture. Then there is Fossar de la Pedrera Park by Beth Galí (1983–1986), one of Barcelona's quiet places, whose symbolism is particularly evident. The majority of these "selective" projects are characterized by a desire to apply a totally new treatment to every urban space, irrespective of whether it is a park, a bridge or a tunnel; architectural design and actual construction enjoy, in this treatment, parity of esteem.

A clear process of development can be traced in Barcelona's squares. The first projects, starting around 1982, were characterized by a reluctance to go beyond the reshaping of an already existing square within a historical urban texture. Examples can be seen in the Gràcia district, or in the old city. Then, in about 1985, there was an increase in the number of more ambitious, larger-scale projects. These were concentrated in the peripheral districts as well as in the less conspicuous central sections. A good example is the Parc de la Creueta del Coll by Martorell, Bohigas and Mackay (1981–1987), with its lake posi-

LA XEMENEIA D'EN FOLCH

Josep Martorell, Oriol Bohigas, David Mackay, Albert Puigdomènech, 1986–1992
Olympic Village, Poble Nou

In 1986 a planning group under Oriol Bohigas took just a few weeks to lay down the basic outlines which were to determine the appearance of the buildings in the Olympic Village. This was a task of far-reaching importance for the development of the city, in view of the fact that it encompassed the reclamation of a considerable length of coastline. A conspicuous feature of the results of this planning is the fact that none of the three basic planning systems which might have been adduced was actually employed in any obvious manner, namely the axial structures of the Beaux-Arts system, the homogeneous layout of the Cerdà plan, or the block system favoured by the rationalists.

The site of the Olympic Village lies behind the Ciutadella and the barracks, occupying the former sites of the Folch and Torras factories and Elies Rogent's docks. The only survival of this huge industrial estate still standing today is the Folch factory's brick chimney, next to one of the large new residential complexes.

tioned alongside a disused quarry; another is the park by the north railway station (1985–1987), with its wonderful landscaped sculptures by Beverly Pepper; and not least the park surrounding the Villa Cecilia, designed by Elías Torres and José Antonio Martínez Lapeña (1982–1986). Many of these public squares are given a quite personal touch by the presence of sculptures.[50] After most of the goals had been achieved, 1990 saw a return to a "minimalist" concept, concentrating on the upgrading of pavements, streetlighting, access routes and road surfacing.

The "selective" construction measures also embrace cultural projects. As representative examples, we shall mention here two works by Jordi Garcés and Enric Soria: the Museu Picasso (1981–1987), the rebuilding of which led to the modernization of some old palaces on the Carrer de Montcada; and the Museu de la Ciència (1979–1980), which was installed in a converted old people's home.[51] Both buildings are models of sensitive "surgery" on historic architecture. In the heart of the old city, the site of a former hospital, the Casa de la Caritat, is being converted into a centre for contemporary art. The two most important elements are the rooms devoted to the theme "La ciudad de las ciudades" by Albert Viaplana and Helio Piñón (1990)[52] and the Museu d'Art Contemporani, designed by the American Richard Meier (1987–1992).

A typical feature influencing current developments in Barcelona – and not only in a positive sense – is the increasing importance of the service sector. Bit by bit the city is being transformed into a large centre of employment, commerce and culture; a city in which there is ever less room for its poorer inhabitants. This phenomenon can of course be discerned in all post-industrial cities, and the result is that certain districts become the exclusive preserve of the tertiary sector. It is not exactly any longer a secret that such one-sided use results in a neighbourhood shorn of all vitality outside normal business hours, in other words in the evenings and on the weekends.

In the smaller-scale world of interior design, too, Barcelona's achievements during the 1980s – as during the period of Modernismo – have been notable for the elevated artistic level characterizing the design of shops and restaurants. Among the earliest establishments to display a really innovative flair were the KGB music bar with its simple, urbane design and the Bijoux cocktail bar with its sumptuous fittings. It was the late 1980s which witnessed the advent of the veritable cult sites of modern design: the Otto Zutz Club, in converted workshops spread over a number of storeys; the Nick Havanna, with its festive, playful ambience; and the Network restaurant, with its cool, sophisticated aesthetic. This list should also find room for a small Chinese restaurant: the Pekín. After

HOTEL DE LAS ARTES

Skidmore, Owings & Merrill;
Frank O. Gehry, 1986–1992
Passeig de Carles I

A component of the comprehensive planning in the run-up to the Olympic Games was a project for two tower blocks by the new Puerto Olímpico. The design for the five-star hotel is due to Bruce Graham from the Chicago firm of Skidmore, Owings & Merrill, an old hand at skyscrapers. The high-rise office building facing the hotel was the work of Iñigo Ortiz and Enrique León.

APARTMENT BLOCK

José Luis Mateo, 1984–1990
Carrer de Bilbao, Poble Nou

that, the level sinks to pure mannerism; only a few places, such as the Zsa Zsa, with its stage-set decor, the neo-traditional Casa Fernández, or the Tragaluz restaurant stand out above the average.

And there we close this survey of the architecture of Barcelona. It is a survey which has tried to embrace both town-planning questions – including the wide-ranging and successful example represented by the Cerdà plan, and the ambitious venture of the Olympics – as well as the smaller-scale world of interior decoration and furnishing. The handling of differing dimensions in the creative shaping of space and environment in Barcelona must strike the eye of the beholder time and again. Nevertheless, there remain numerous challenges facing the city and its surroundings. These include sensitive landscape management, with the aim of preserving existing landscapes, creating new habitats and healing the wounds caused by uncontrolled building in recent decades; the provision of suitable premises for cultural activities; the control of the current impetuous invasion of the city by the service sector, and the struggle against the standardization of multifarious urban life by monotonous office blocks; and finally, the improvement of living conditions by upgrading a large proportion of the housing, long an object of neglect. Finally, Barcelona must somehow manage to improve the quality of its life and to continue along the road to modernity, without at the same time losing the features of a city constructed from small fragments with much attention to detail, a living city, in which there is a place for all social classes.

OLYMPIC STADIUM

Federico Correa, Alfonso Milà, Carles Buxadé,
Joan Margarit, Vittorio Gregotti, Pedro Ibáñez,
1986–1989
Montjuïc

Barcelona's Olympic Stadium, built in 1929 on Montjuïc, was intended as the venue for the 1936 Olympics. The decision on that occasion, however, went in favour of Berlin. An Olímpiada Popular was planned as an alternative for Barcelona in protest against Hitler's policies: Jews and Communists were banned from competing for Germany in the official Olympics. However these alternative Olympics were also thwarted at the last minute by General Franco's putsch. At last, in 1992, this stadium belatedly came into its own. Recognizing the significance of the site, the architects retained the historic façade and entrance when planning the necessary enlargements. By lowering the level of the arena, space for extra grandstand seating was created, giving the stadium a capacity of 60,000. In the course of the enlargement, the opportunity was of course taken to carry out a series of rebuilding measures in order to provide an infrastructure measuring up to today's communications requirements as well as to modern standards of seating comfort and visibility. Today, Barcelona's Olympic Stadium is once more one of the most modern and imposing sporting arenas in the world.

PALAU SANT JORDI

Arata Isozaki, 1984–1990
Montjuïc

Immediately adjacent to the Olympic Stadium, this indoor arena is without doubt one of the hallmarks of Barcelona, the Olympic City of 1992.

The hall was conceived as a multi-purpose structure; it has a 200-metre track, and can also be used as an ice rink. Apart from hosting sporting events, it is also suitable for use as an exhibition or concert hall. The spectators' entrance is situated on the large plaza between the Olympic Stadium and the Palau, while the competitors', press and service entrances are on the lower level on the south side.

The construction of the dome was solved in a spectacular manner, it being first assembled in its entirety on the ground, and then lifted by hydraulic winches into its final position. Its shape is intended as a reflection of the shape of Montjuïc itself.

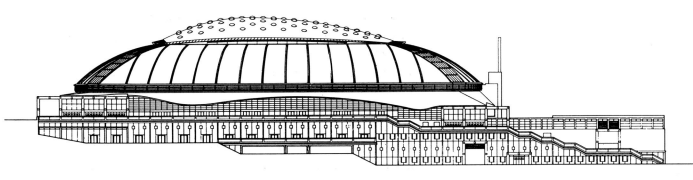

PALAU SANT JORDI

Multi-purpose hall and plaza

TELECOMMUNICATIONS TOWER

Norman Foster, 1989–1992
Collserola

The design of the tower is in accordance with Norman Foster's philosophy of achieving the maximum possible effect with the minimum possible structural effort. The starting-point of the construction is a mast of relatively small diameter, reminiscent of a ship's mast or a flagpole. Three vertical steel girders, spaced at angles of 120°, support the core of the structure, while three cables are anchored in the mountain. This system of support and tension forms the skeleton, in which the various levels and platforms are suspended.

The basic shape – an equilateral triangle with convex sides – was deliberately chosen to offer the least possible wind resistance, while at the same time providing the maximum possible resistance to vibrations, twisting and swaying. The degree of attention devoted to safety and servicing aspects is worthy of note. Thus the lift shafts, staircases and cable ducts are placed on the exterior of the tower, in order to facilitate access. The main tension cables were constructed in such a way as to allow the removal of up to one-third of each cable without jeopardizing the stability of the tower.

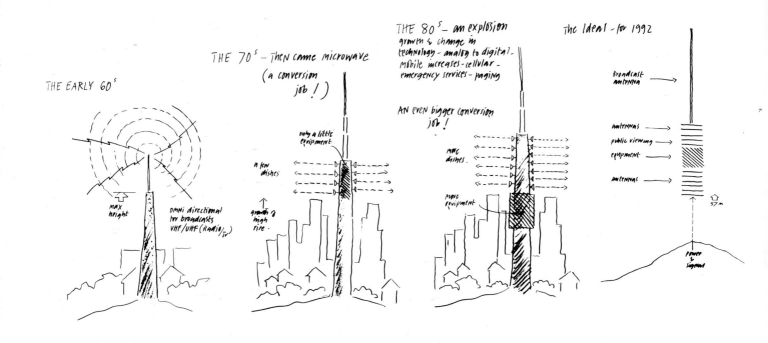

"GRUPO ROSA" WAREHOUSE

Alfredo Arribas, Miguel Morte, 1989–1990
Longitudinal 7, parcela 19F, Mercabarna

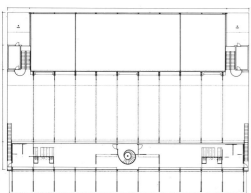

TORRES DE AVILA

Alfredo Arribas, Javier Mariscal, Miguel
Morte, 1989–1990
Poble Espanyol, Avinguda del Marquès
de Comillas

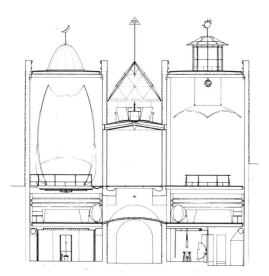

TORRES DE AVILA

Bar in Moon Tower (left), Bar in Sun Tower

Gentlemen's toilet: anteroom; staircase

This reconstruction of the Avila city gate
came into existence on the occasion of
the 1929 World Exhibition, forming the entrance and exit to the tranquil Poble Espanyol with its reconstructions of Spain's most
beautiful buildings.
Standing in the main square of the "Spanish village", the visitor's attention is first
caught only by the glass pyramid between
the massive towers. Entering the building
itself, however, one steps into a world of
visual adventure. The austere articulation
of the outer walls led Alfredo Arribas and
Javier Mariscal to the idea of a Sun Tower
and a Moon Tower. The martial character
of the fortified walls is transformed in the
interior into an interplay of the sexes: the
Torre del Sol symbolizes the male principle, the Torre de la Luna the female.
The Sun Tower is open, clear and imposing: a bar snuggles into the rotunda, while
above, a circular opening in the ceiling
allows one to see into the bright space at
the top of the tower. Beneath the roof, in
the middle of a rectangular vault, a ball
moves up and down, projecting points of
light on to the walls. The soft furniture is
an earthy brown, as is the rest of the room.
The Moon Tower is laid out in a contrapuntal manner: above the bar rotunda
there is, not an opening as in the Sun
Tower, but a circular gallery. The seating
in this gallery is surrounded by an envelop-
ing white wall which opens up to the
centre of the room. This wall can be transformed into a computer-controlled, plane-
tarium-like, night sky. Illuminated optical
fibres give the outer wall the appearance
of being covered in illuminated ivy. Mariscal's inexhaustible symbol-games crop up
in countless variations throughout the
building and on the roof terrace, on which
are structures decorated with the insignia
of sun and moon.

NETWORK

Alfredo Arribas, Eduardo Samsó, 1986–1987
Avinguda Diagonal 616

A large round hole links the three storeys of the Network café, bar and restaurant like some communicating tube. Television monitors, showing without interruption such films as "Blade Runner", "Mad Max" or "Brazil", characterize this post-nuclear ambience.

The Otto Zutz discotheque is situated in the premises of a disused factory; additional structures have been built to match the industrial architecture.

OTTO ZUTZ

Guillem Bonet, Alicia Núñez,
Jordi Parcerisas, 1985
Carrer de Lincoln 15

NICK HAVANNA

Eduardo Samsó, Peret (graphics), 1985–1986
Carrer del Rosselló 208

The design of the Nick Havanna bar was a
breakthrough for Eduardo Samsó. The
high points, so to speak, of the long, low
room are the effects created by the play of
light of a dome and a monitor-wall showing current news, film sequences and
video clips. Other furnishings include fax
machines and a slot machine decorated
with paperbacks.

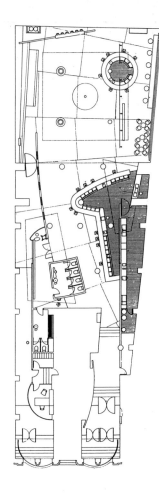

ZSA ZSA

Daniel Freixes, Vicente Miranda, 1988–1989
Carrer del Rosselló 156

The special features of this music bar are
its skilful use of lighting, and the large, re-
flecting plates of glass which effectively
distract attention from the tunnel-like
shape of the room. The wall-carpet collage of classical patterns is by Peret.

VELVET

Alfredo Arribas, Miguel Morte, 1987
Carrer de Balmes 161

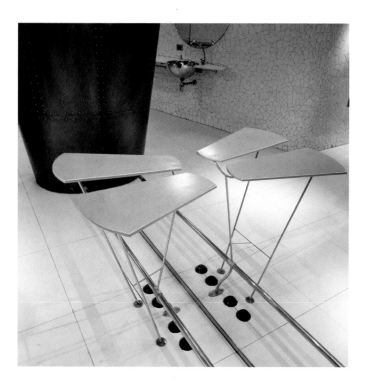

MARCEL

Eduardo Samsó, 1987
Avinguda Diagonal 472

LURDES BERGADA (right)

Eduardo Samsó, 1989
Avinguda Diagonal 609–615

When designing his projects, Eduardo Samsó attaches particular importance to a harmonious and intelligent interplay of user, layout and furniture. He prefers unprocessed, sometimes also faulty materials with their natural colours and surface properties, which he shapes into soft, rounded forms and effective combinations. However, he is no less keen to hark back to Catalan tradition, for example, by cladding the walls with mosaics made from ceramic fragments, as in the "Marcel" hairdressing salon in the Boulevard Rosa shopping centre. For reasons of space, the salon's ground floor has no more than a reception area and a spiral staircase, which leads down to the actual hairdressing area in the basement.

A less attractive area in the Avinguda Diagonal is the site of the "Lurdes Bergadà" fashion shop: the premises are small, with floorboards, blue-velvet curtains and just a few carefully placed items of furniture – the whole being reminiscent of Japanese interiors.

CASA BERENGUER D'AGUILAR
MUSEU PICASSO

Jordi Garcés, Enric Sòria, 1981–1987
Carrer de Montcada 15

The house of the aristocrat, Joan Berenguer d'Aguilar was built in the 15th century, the architect Marc Safont probably being involved in its construction. Since the 1960s it has been used to display works by Pablo Picasso. It has since been altered and enlarged by Garcés and Sòria, who incorporated adjacent palaces for the purpose. The result is highly successful.

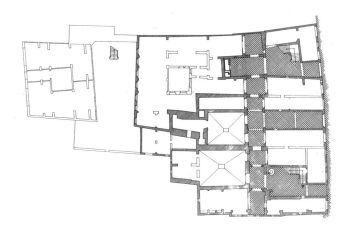

MUSEU DE LA CIENCIA

Josep Domènech i Estapà, 1904–1909; Jordi Garcés, Enric Sòria, 1979–1980; Alfredo Arribas, Miguel Morte, Javier Mariscal, 1989 Carrer de Teodor Roviralta 55

This museum of science, planned in the late 1970s, is housed in the former old people's home, Amparo de Santa Lucia, and was designed by Josep Domènech i Estapà. To the long frontage of the original building Garcés and Sòria have added an extension which preserves the lines of the fine old façade, reinterpreting its layout in a highly successful manner. It is a prime example of how to extend a façade. Exemplary, too, is the way the museum is fitted out. The approach is exclusively sensory, beginning with installations illustrating optical phenomena, or experiments in kinetics, and going on to the varied olfactory experience of the "sniffing bar". Everything is arranged to withstand rough treatment. In 1989, Arribas, Morte and Mariscal set up "El Clic dels Nens" on the ground floor – a colourful paradise of learning by playing, intended for the museum's younger visitors (right).

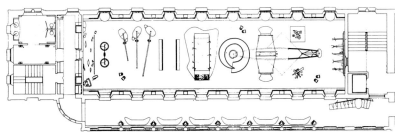

HIGH SCHOOL

Joan Amigó Barriga, 1906–1919; Enric
Miralles, Carme Pinós, 1984–1986
Badalona, Barcelona

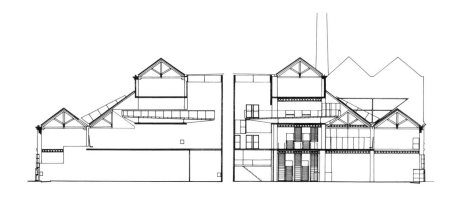

This building is the former La Llauna factory, converted for use as a high school. The work is marked by respect for the existing industrial architecture, while at the same time clearly showing deconstructivist elements. Enric Miralles and Carme Pinós have pursued this style in a rigorous and creative manner. The rooms and fittings deliberately reflect the aggressive aesthetic of the streets and the outskirts of the city.

INSTITUT MARTI I POL

Eduard Bru, José Luis Mateo, 1981–1983
Sta. Coloma de Gramanet, Barcelona

"DE LA CONCEPCION" SCHOOL

Pep Zazurca, 1988–1990
Carrer Bruc 102

JOSEP MARIA JUJOL SCHOOL

Josep Maria Jujol, 1916–1918; Jaume Bach,
Gabriel Mora, 1984–1987
Carrer de la Riera de Sant Miquel 39

Like the high school in the former La
Llauna factory, this one is also in converted industrial premises. Josep Maria
Jujol built the workshops, in which safes
were manufactured, for the industrialist
Señor Mañach. Today they are used as an
assembly hall and recreation area.

TEATRE NACIONAL DE CATALUNYA

Ricardo Bofill, Taller de Arquitectura,
1989–1992
Plaça de les Glòries

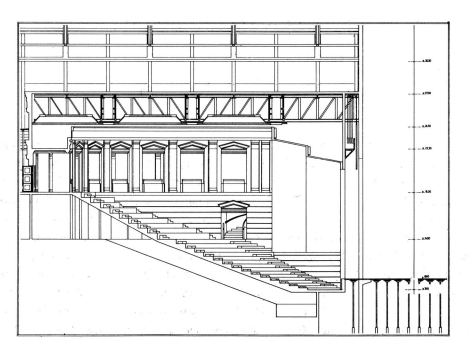

MUSEU D'ARTE CONTEMPORANI

Richard Meier, Thomas Phifer, 1987–1992
Carrer Montalegre 7, Plaça del Angels

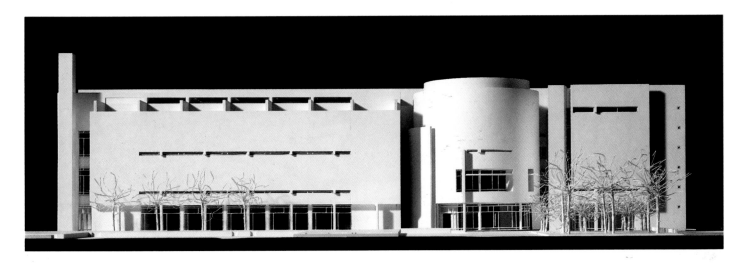

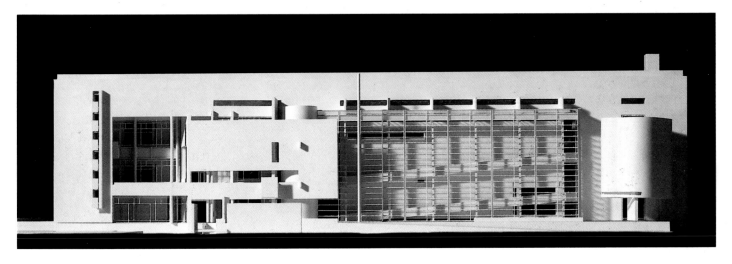

Currently under construction on the Plaça de les Glòries – the intersection of the major traffic arteries Gran Via de les Corts Catalanes, Avinguda Diagonal and Avinguda Meridiana – is Barcelona's largest centre of the arts, the Teatre Nacional de Catalunya, which consists of two self-contained components: a concert hall based on plans by Rafael Moneo and a theatre building by Ricardo Bofill.

Bofill's design is based on three tracts: a bright concourse with palm-lined entrances, the so-called Casa, and the theatre itself, which is planned to seat 1500. The auditorium is semi-circular, with rows of seats in steep tiers. There are no galleries or boxes.

The Museu d'Art Contemporani in Barcelona's old city is intended as a bridge between the historic Casa de la Caritat, whose architectural history goes back to the 14th century and the contemporary art to be displayed here. The American architect Richard Meier's design shows an unabashedly modern structure, which, unlike Ricardo Bofill's theatre, has no need of stylistic citations. Instead the mediation is achieved via clearly defined volumes and balanced façades. The plans herald a masterpiece, taking up the trail of the High Museum of Art in Atlanta, Georgia and the Museum für Kunsthandwerk in Frankfurt am Main.

APPENDIX

NOTES

1 Círculo de Economía, Gestión o Caos. El area metropolitana de Barcelona, Ariel, Barcelona, 1973

2 Josep-Maria Montaner, La modernizacío de l'utillatge mental de l'arquitectura a Catalunya [1714–1859], Institut d'Estudis Catalans, Barcelona, 1990

3 Manuel Arranz, Mestres d'obres i Fusters. La construcció a Barcelona en el segle XVIII, Collegi d'Aparelladors i Arquitectes Tècnics de Barcelona, Barcelona, 1991

4 Pere Hereu "L'edifici de la Universitat, testimoni de l'urbanisme del seu moment históric" in Elias Rogent i la Universitat de Barcelona, "Generalitat" de Catalunya/Universitat de Barcelona, Barcelona, 1988

5 Albert Garcia i Espuche and Manuel Guàrdia i Bassols, Espai i societat a la Barcelona pre-industrial, La Magrana, Barcelona, 1986

6 Ildefonso Cerdà, Teoría General de la Urbanización. Reforma y "Eixample" de Barcelona, Instituto de Estudios Fiscales, Barcelona, 1968; and 2 C. Construcción de la ciudad nos. 6–7, 1977, dedicated to Cerdà. Josep-Maria Montaner, "The Cerdà Plan" in Catalonia Culture no. 3, 1987

7 Oriol Bohigas, Barcelona. Entre el barraquisme i el Pla Cerdà, Edicions 62, Barcelona, 1963

8 Manuel de Solà-Morales [Laboratorio de Urbanismo], Los "Eixample" s I. El "Eixample" de Barcelona, Escola Tècnica Superior d'Arquitectura, Barcelona, 1978

9 Albert Garcia Espuche, El quadrat d'or. Centre de la Barcelona modernista, Olimpiada Cultural y Lunwerg, Barcelona, 1990

10 Manuel Guàrdia, Albert Garcia Espuche, José Luís Oyon and Francisco Javier Molins, "La dimensió urbana" in Arquitectura i Ciutat a l'exposició universal de Barcelona 1888, Universitat Politècnica de Catalunya, Barcelona, 1988

11 José Corredor-Matheos and Josep-Maria Montaner, Arquitectura industrial en Cataluña. De 1732 a 1929, Caja de Barcelona, Barcelona, 1984

12 Francesc Cabana, Assumpció Feliu, Can Torras dels ferros: 1876–1985, Barcelona, 1987

13 Jeroni Martorell, Estructuras de ladrillo y hierro atirantado en la arquitectura catalana moderna, Anuario de Arquitectos, Barcelona, 1910

14 Pere Hereu, L'Arquitectura d'Elies Rogent, Collegi d'Arquitectes de Catalunya, Barcelona, 1986

15 Cuadernos de Arquitectura nos. 52–53, 1963, dedicated to "Domènech i Montaner"; A. A. V. V. Lluís Domènech i Montaner. En el 50e Aniversari de la seva mort. 1850–1923, Lluís Carulla, Barcelona, 1973

16 Mireia Freixa, El modernismo en España, Cátedra, Madrid, 1986

17 Henry-Russell Hitchcock, Arquitectura de los siglos XIX y XX, Cátedra, Madrid, 1981

18 Xavier Güell, Antoni Gaudí, Gustavo Gili, Barcelona, 1986

19 Le Corbusier, J. Gomis und J. Prats, Gaudí, Editorial de Arquitectos de Cataluña y Baleares, Barcelona, 1975

20 Joan Bassegoda Nonell, Los maestros de obras de Barcelona, Tècnicos Asociados, Barcelona, 1973; Josep-Maria Montaner, L'ofici de l'arquitectura, Universitat Politècnica de Catalunya, Barcelona, 1983

21 Oriol Bohigas, Reseña y Catálogo de la arquitectura modernista, Lumen, Barcelona, 1973

22 Ignasi de Solà-Morales, Joan Rubió i Bellver y la fortuna del gaudinismo, Colegio Oficial de Arquitectos de Cataluña y Baleares, Barcelona, 1975

23 Quaderns nos. 179–180, 1989, Barcelona, dedicated to "Josep Maria Jujol, arquitecte. 1879–1949"; Ignasi de Solà-Morales, Jujol, Polígrafa, Barcelona, 1990; Oriol Bohigas, "Josep Maria Jujol" in Once Arquitectos, La Gaya Ciencia, Barcelona, 1976

24 Josep-Maria Montaner, "Puig i Cadafalch, la legitimació de l'arquitectura", in EL PAIS, Barcelona, 7 December 1989

25 Quaderns d'Arquitectura i Urbanisme no. 113, 1976, dedicated to "Noucentisme: la arquitectura de la ciudad"

26 Josep-Maria Rovira, Xavier Güell und Xavier Pouplana, Memòria Renaixentista en l'arquitectura catalana [1920–1950], Collegi Oficial d'Arquitectes de Catalunya i Baleares, Barcelona, 1983

27 Ignasi de Solà-Morales, La Exposición Internacional de Barcelona 1914–1929: Arquitectura y Ciudad, Feria de Barcelona, Barcelona, 1985

28 Nicolau Maria Rubió i Tudurí, El jardín meridional. Estudio de su trazado y plantación, Salvat, Barcelona, 1934; and Nicolau Maria Rubió, Acta, culture committee of the Colegio Oficial de Aparejadores y Arquitectos Técnicos, Murcia, 1984

29 Francesc Roca, El Plà Macià, La Magrana, Barcelona, 1977

30 Francesc Roca, Ignasi de Solà-Morales (eds.) A. C./GATEPAC. 1931–1937, Gustavo Gili, Barcelona, 1975

31 Oriol Bohigas, Arquitectura española de la Segunda Repúblicam, Tusquets, Barcelona, 1970

32 Ernesto Katzenstein, Gustavo Natanson and Hugo Schuartzman, Antonio Bonet. Arquitectura y urbanismo en el Rio de la Plata y España, Espacio, Buenos Aires, 1985

33 A. A. V. V., Antoni de Moragas Gallissà. Homenatge, Gustavo Gili/FAD, Barcelona, 1989

34 Carlos Fochs (ed.) José Antonio Coderch de Sentmenat. 1913–1984, "Generalitat" de Catalunya, Barcelona, 1988

35 Antonio de Moragas, "Deu anys del Grup R" in Serra d'Or nos. 11–12, 1961, Barcelona

36 Oriol Bohigas "Una posible Escuela de Barcelona" in Contra una arquitectura adjectivada, Seix Barral, Barcelona, 1982

37 Josep-Maria Montaner "España" in Leonardo Benévolo, Historia de la Arquitectura Moderna, Gustavo Gili, Barcelona, 1982

38 Helio Piñon, Arquitecturas catalanas, La Gaya Ciencia, Barcelona, 1977

39 Josep-Maria Montaner "Surveying Catalan Architecture, 1951–1987" in Sites no. 20, New York, 1988

40 A. A. V. V. Plans i projectes per a Barcelona. 1981–1982, Ajuntament de Barcelona, Barcelona, 1983; and Oriol Bohigas, Reconstrucció de Barcelona, Edicions 62, Barcelona, 1985

41 Josep-Maria Montaner "Barcelone ou la course du siècle" in Metropol 90, Pavillon de l'Arsenal, Paris, 1990

42 Franco Rella "Figure nel laberinto. La metamorfosi di una metafora" in Peter Eisenman, La fine del classico, CLUVA, Venice, 1987

43 A. A. V. V. La ciutat i el 92, Holsa y Olímpiada Cultural, Barcelona, 1990

44 Claude Lévi-Strauss, Tristes Trópicos, Editorial Universitaria de Buenos Aires, Buenos Aires, 1970

45 Martorell, Bohigas, Mackay, Puigdomènech, Vila olímpica. Transformación de un frente marítimo, Gustavo Gili, Barcelona, 1988; A & V. Monografías de Arquitectura y Vivienda, no. 22, dedicated to "Barcelona 1992. Vila olímpica", Madrid, 1990; and Lotus internacional no. 67, dedicated to "I grandi progetti di transformazione", Milan, 1990

46 William J. R. Curtis (introduction), Carlos Ferrater, Gustavo Gili, Barcelona, 1989

47 Josep-Maria Montaner "Palau Sant Jordi. Valoración de un gran premio" in Diseño Interior no. 6, Madrid, 1991

48 Quaderns nos. 188–189, "Guia d'Arquitectura contemporània. Barcelona i la seva àrea territorial, 1928–1900", 1991

49 Arees de Nova Centralitat. New downtowns in Barcelona, Ajuntament de Barcelona, Barcelona, 1987

50 Barcelona. Espais i escultures (1982–1986), Ajuntament de Barcelona, 1987

51 Oriol Bohigas (introduction), Gracés/Sòria, Gustavo Gili, Barcelona, 1987

52 Josep-Maria Montaner, "The optimism of geometry" in Sites no. 24, New York, 1992

BIBLIOGRAPHY

Josep Emili Hernàndez-Cros, Gabriel Mora, Xavier Pouplana, Arquitectura de Barcelona, Collegi d'Arquitectes de Catalunya, Barcelona, 1989

Catàleg del Patrimoni Arquitectònic Històrico-Artistic de la Ciutat de Barcelona, Ajuntament de Barcelona

Richard C. Levene, Fernando Márquez Cecilia, Antonio Ruiz Barbarin, Arquitectura espanola contemporánea. 1975–1990, El Croquis, Madrid, 1989

La Arquitectura de los años cincuenta en Barcelona, Ayuntamiento de Barcelona, 1987

Xavier Güell (ed.), Spanische Architektur der achtziger Jahre, Berlin, 1990

Volker Fischer, Eduard Bru i Bistuer, Neue Architekturtendenzen, Barcelona, Berlin, 1991

Oriol Bohigas, Peter Buchanan, Vittorio Magnago Lampugnani, Barcelona. Arquitectura y Ciudad 1980–1992, Barcelona, 1992

Catalunya, la fàbrica d'Espanya. Un segle d'industrialització catalana. 1833–1936, Ajuntament de Barcelona, Generalitat de Catalunya, Barcelona, 1985

Design in Catalonia, BCD Barcelona Design Centre, 1988

Lluís Domènech i Montaner i el Director d'Orquestra, Fundació Caixa Barcelona, 1989

Exposició Universal de Barcelona. Llibre del Centenari 1888–1988, Barcelona, 1988

Carlos Flores, Gaudí, Jujol y el Modernismo Catalan, Madrid, 1982

Rainer Zerbst, Antoni Gaudí, Cologne, 1988 (English Edition)

José Llinàs, Jordi Sarrà, Josep Maria Jujol, Cologne, 1992

Jaume de Puig, Antoni González, Raquel Lacuesta, Josep M. Moreno, M. Gràcia Salva, Ramon Manent, El Palau Güell, Diputacio de Barcelona, 1990

Antoni Sàbat, Palau de la Música Catalana, Barcelona, 1974

Josep Puig i Cadafalch, l'arquitectura entre la casa i la ciutat, Fundació Caixa de Pensions, 1989

Peter Dutli, Jörg Esefeld, Pierre Kreis, Neue Stadträume in Barcelona. Stadterneuerung durch Plätze, Parkanlagen, Straßenräume und Skulpturen, Zurich, 1991

ARCHITECTS

INDEX OF BUILDINGS

PHOTO CREDITS

Arxiu Administratiu de l'Ajuntament de Barcelona: 24

Arxiu Capitular de la Catedral de Barcelona: 14/15

Arxiu Mas, Barcelona: 75, 76, 81, 83, 84, 89, 90, 93, 97, 100, 105, 113b., 116, 120, 124, 130, 131, 144/145, 148, 151, 153, 180, 188, 198/199, 202, 204, 205

Bibliothek der Landesgewerbeanstalt Nürnberg: 9

Lluís Casals, Barcelona: 45a., 196, 271, 279, 285, 286, 287

Francesc Català-Roca, Barcelona: 42, 150, 160, 200 a., 201, 203, 208/209, 211, 212, 218, 219, 222, 223, 224, 225, 226, 228, 229, 230, 231, 238, 242, 278

Cb-foto, Julio Conill, Barcelona: 194, 195

Collegi d'Arquitectes de Catalunya, Barcelona: 38/39, 45 b., 54 b., 200 b.

ESTO Photographics/Jock Pottle, Mamaroneck, NY: 289

Firo-Foto, Barcelona: 11, 89, 134

Ferran Freixa, Barcelona: 67, 68/69, 240 b., 241 a., 255, 256, 257, 258, 282, 283, 284

Peter Gössel, Nuremberg: 243 b.

Jordi Gumí, Barcelona: 214, 216, 220, 227

Hovisa, Barcelona: 250

Institut Municipal d'Història, Barcelona: 10, 12, 16/17, 18, 19, 20, 26, 27, 28/29, 31, 44, 46 b., 48, 54 a., 57, 60, 62, 64, 65, 71, 88, 95, 110/111, 112, 114, 115, 158/159, 161, 162 b., 164, 166, 176, 177, 178/179, 182, 184, 187, 190, 192, 197

Jordi Isern, Barcelona: 56

Lurdes Jansana, Barcelona: 243 a., 253

Ramon Manent, Mataró: 78, 85

Museu d'Història de la Ciutat de Barcelona: 22

Roger-Viollet, Paris: 34, 35, 41, 50/51, 52

François René Roland, Verrue: 77, 82

Jordi Sarrà, Barcelona: front cover, 8, 30, 32/33, 40, 43, 46 a., 47, 49, 58, 59, 70, 72, 74, 79, 80, 92, 96, 98, 101, 102, 103, 104, 106, 107, 108, 109, 113 a., 114, 117, 118, 119, 121, 122/123, 125, 126, 127, 128/129, 140/141, 142, 143, 145, 146/147, 149, 152, 154, 155, 156, 157, 162 a., 163, 165/back cover, 167, 168, 169, 172/173, 174, 186, 198 a., 199, 232, 233, 246, 254/255, 259, 261, 264/265, 266, 270, 272, 273, 275, 276, 277, 280, 281

Hisao Suzuki, Barcelona: 62/63, 132, 133, 136, 137, 138, 139, 234/235, 241 b., 262, 263, 267, 268, 269, 274 b.

Plans, drawings and photographs of models were kindly placed at our disposal by the architects, the Arxiu Administratiu de l'Ajuntament de Barcelona and the Collegi d'Arquitectes de Catalunya, Barcelona.

Our contacts with the archives, the photographers and the architects were helped by the enthusiastic support of Frigga Finkentey and Isabel Martín.